GOD OF THE IMPOSSIBLE
The Healing of Anna Joy

by

SUSAN PETERS

GOD OF THE IMPOSSIBLE
The Healing of Anna Joy

Acknowledgment

There are so many I want to thank for helping me with this book. First and foremost, I want to thank Jesus for apprehending my heart, healing and delivering me and my family and for giving me the awesome opportunity to preach the Word.

Next, I want to thank my husband Marty who has always been my biggest cheerleader. He has taught me the Word of God and pushed me to stand strong and unwavering in life's battles. I also want to thank my amazing girls: Jessica, Brooke, Anna Joy and Lindsey. I could not be more proud of the confident, godly, young women leaders they have become. Thank you for your support and for allowing Jesus to mold you and use you to advance His Kingdom.

To my sister Dr. Debby Yoder, my mom Hazel Merz, my dad Len Yoder and Dan and Mercedes Peters, my in-laws: I am blessed to have your love, support and hard work that made this project possible.

To Marisol and Bill Curtiss, Rachel Logan, and Debbie Wallace: Thank you for your many hours in preparing and editing this book.

To all my wonderful friends: I am so honored and blessed that you believe in me. You provide such vital emotional and prayer support. Thank you for walking alongside me in declaring the truth that God truly is the God of the impossible, the God of complete healing.

I want to give special acknowledgement to Jimmy and Laura Seibert, my pastors and long time friends. They have mentored me, prayed for me and opened many opportunities to serve with them, which has been the delight of my heart. Your commitment to holiness, loving people, preaching the Word without compromise, and living in authentic relationships inspires me.

Table of Contents

Foreword

My husband and I had known Marty and Susan for several years before Anna Joy's birth. We rejoiced with them when their third daughter was born, and then were dismayed to hear the doctors' terrible reports about her disease and all the devastating effects it would have on their baby girl. In the days ahead, we saw the evidence of her disease ourselves. Having raised six of our own children, we knew what was "normal" in a baby. As the months passed, we recognized that Anna Joy was far from normal. Her eyes never focused on anything, she didn't respond to any kind of sound, and her little body was limp and lifeless, not constantly moving like most babies' bodies did.

We knew the Peters were firm believers in the healing power of God. We watched in amazement as they walked out their beliefs by carefully speaking over Anna God's words of faith, month after month, though the evidence of Anna Joy's devastating condition was right before their eyes. It was almost as if they could not see that she was deaf and blind because they were looking at her with eyes of faith.

One evening Susan called and asked if my husband, Chris, and I would join them at their home to proclaim in prayer over Anna Joy that her healing had been accomplished. They knew in their spirits that she was healed but were frustrated that her healing had not yet manifested. We held hands with them and prayed a simple prayer, thanking God that her healing was finished.

About a month later, I was sitting in the back of church during an evening service, watching Susan struggle as she tried to control her squirming girls, since Marty was not there to help. I approached Susan and asked if I could hold Anna Joy for her. I brought her back to my seat with me and began refocusing on the pastor's message, but something about Anna drew my attention to her. I gasped in amazement and joy as I saw her eyes focus on mine and her mouth respond in a smile. She was moving around, just like a normal little baby! Without even thinking, I ran up to where Susan was seated and whispered, "When did this happen?" She smiled sweetly and said, "She began manifesting her healing a few days ago!" I was overcome with laughing and weeping over the miracle of Anna Joy's healing.

Of course, Jesus, our Healer, is the real hero in Anna Joy's story. But I know in my heart, because I was there, that Anna Joy Peters, a completely healed, beautiful, normal young lady, is blessed because she has parents who looked at her with eyes of faith, who stood believing in the face of contradicting evidence that their baby was healed and perfect. As the Scriptures say, "Blessed are they who did not see, and yet believed." (John 20:29)

As Christians, most of us struggle with the fact that God does not always heal. I believe this cannot help but influence the way we pray for those who need healing. If I find my faith in God's healing provision wavering, I need only recall Anna Joy's miraculous story to strengthen my faith in our Jehovah Rapha. That's why her story is so important to the Body of Christ.

I hope those who are reading this book will share Anna's story with many others who need to know that our God can and still does perform healings that are so supernatural, so outrageous, that we are encouraged again to believe for the impossible.

Becky Weatherly
Waco, Texas

Foreword

The "God of the Impossible" is about an amazing family's journey of faith of which I've been thankful to be a part. Anna Joy holds a very special place in my heart since she was named after me. What an honor it is to share my name with someone so beautiful and who is a true miracle of God.

God brought Marty and Susan in my life at the perfect time. They had such a passion for God's Word in the realm of healing. I had read passages in the Bible where Jesus healed but had my own doubts about whether God would heal today. Sometimes past circumstances and hurts keep us from seeing God's ability to heal. This was certainly true for me when at thirteen years old I watched my mother die of cancer.

I fully believe that with God there are no coincidences. Not only did Susan and I attend the same church, but we were both pregnant at the same time and had daughters in the same grade at school. Needless to say we became good friends. God knew how critical this friendship would be for me to lay hold of His healing power for the unseen battles I would face in the days ahead.

During her pregnancy with Anna Joy, Susan was always sharing about God's ability to heal people today. I knew God had healed, and knew He could heal, but had been taught differently than what she shared with me. Every time I went to her house she was watching videos on God's healing for today or listening to people share testimonies of how God had healed them from incurable diseases.

Susan had no idea that she and Marty were going to be in a battle for the very life and health of their own baby. She was constantly filling her heart with God's healing Word, allowing God to instill His truth in them. It was the foundation they were going to need to win this battle. Hebrews 10:35-36 says, *"So do not throw away your confidence; it will be richly rewarded. You need to persevere so that when you have done the will of God, you will receive what He has promised."*

When Anna Joy was born with this devastating disease, Marty and Susan did just what Hebrews 10:35-36 declares. During the next year they saw no "natural" results, but they never wavered and did not throw away their confidence in the Lord.

Susan called me with the news from the doctors and said, "I am only going to say this once so you will know how to pray, and after that you will only hear me say what God says about my baby". It was hard for me at times because in my limited understanding, I often thought Susan was in denial.

But as her friend I had committed to stay the course and fight this with them to the end.

In the months that followed I had the privilege of keeping Jessica and Brooke during Anna Joy's many doctor appointments. When Susan would pick up the girls she would only speak positively about Anna Joy, even though the test results were not what they needed to be. Whenever someone asked how Anna Joy was, her response was always the same, "I believe she is healed by the stripes of Jesus." She was practicing one of the most powerful principles in the Bible.

She and Marty were constantly *calling those things that are not as though they are."* As a result, Anna Joy is a testimony of the goodness and faithfulness of God and His Word. She is a special gift from God.

Seeing the Anna Joy miracle watered the seeds in my own heart and now years later my own passion and faith in God's healing power has never been stronger. As I shared before, I didn't know that my own battle for healing would follow. In December of 2007 I was told I had breast cancer. I know that as I continue to declare His Word that I will walk in perfect health. A recent blood test revealed that there is no cancer in my body!

The Bible says that people perish because they lack knowledge. The Gospel is one of power and comfort. The very nature of the Gospel is to solve problems and turn lives around. Not long after Anna Joys healing my own sister was dying in the hospital from a rare pneumonia. I stayed in her hospital room reading this book cover to cover. I declared life and health over my sister and would only allow positive confessions to be spoken over her. She is alive and well today and the doctors told her she is a miracle too!

As you read this powerful story, allow the principles of God's Word to change your life and your circumstances. This message will not only stir up your faith, but it will cause you to soar to new heights in your own walk with the Lord! Wherever you are on your journey cling to God's Word for the "*Eternal's eyes dart here and there over the whole world, as He exerts His power on behalf of those who are devoted to Him.*" 2 Chronicles 16:9.

Anna Rambeau
Waco, Texas

Introduction

"She will have no motor skills, no hearing, and will be blind. She has a devastating disease which happened in utero, and it is irreversible. There is no hope for her. She will do nothing but drool like a six week old baby." I'll never forget hearing those words in the Neonatal Intensive Care Unit when our third child Anna Joy was born. I could hardly breathe or take in the words. I kept thinking, "There's a mistake. He is not talking about my baby." The shock and disbelief my husband and I expressed in the hospital seemed to make the neonatologist explain ever more deliberately how her brain was severely damaged and why she would never run and play like her two older sisters. The doctors ran numerous tests and brain scans, and did blood work to confirm the diagnosis. Her liver and spleen were enlarged, her platelet count was so low she was at hemorrhaging level, and there were massive calcifications on her brain, as well as other complications. Since many of our friends and family were in their childbearing years, the staff had to put signs on the hospital door warning visitors of possible infection because Cytomegalic Inclusion disease is very contagious to pregnant women and those with immune deficiencies.

Before we left the NICU, we signed up for the Clara Center for the Blind, and scheduled the MHMR (Mental Health Mental Retardation) Center to come to our house for regular therapy. We were sent to Cook Children's Hospital in a larger city. I'll never forget seeing the sign on the door that read "Infectious Diseases of Infants." It opened to a beautiful large office with lots of seating and examination rooms; however, no one was there that day except us. I wondered why it was so empty until suddenly it hit me. This office specialized in infectious diseases and that meant we had to be isolated from other patients.

These doctors specialized in Cytomegalic Inclusion disease and confirmed the neonatologist's diagnosis after conducting their own test. They held up the brain scan and for the first time I realized how big of a miracle we really needed. When they had shown us the previous scan in the hospital, I saw holes and thought they were the nose and eye sockets, and the ear holes. But today I realized that the scan was only of her brain. Those holes explained why they said there was no hope for healing. I don't remember a lot from that time at Cook Children's except that I was so glad my sister-in-law, Suzanne, was there to ask questions that I could not think of at the time. She was so calm and comforting. She had begun following Jesus years before, and was now a strong support for us while we balanced our need for medical help with our believing for a miracle. The specialist at Cook Children's Hospital wanted to inject experimental drugs into Anna Joy for research to help develop medicines for future patients. However, there was a long list of negative effects these drugs could have on our daughter, and they would not help her at all. We told the doctors no, and said that we were followers of Jesus, so we believed God could heal her. We took our baby home.

Of course, we continued to go to the doctor. At first, we went three times a week for hours at a time. She often had to go in for platelets, and each time they put us in an isolation room so as not to infect anyone else. One time they did not have another office or waiting room available, so they put us in the storage room with all the old files to keep us isolated. At times like these, I remember driving home and crying so hard that I would have to pull the car over. But even when I hurt for my baby and all that we were going through, deep in my spirit I knew God was a miraculous God and He could heal Anna Joy.

My husband and I had both begun following Jesus in college. As a married couple, we were growing in our faith by going to church, and learning to pray and study our Bibles. We also had developed deep friendships with other believers. Together we believed in a supernatural God who heals and performs miracles today. But we had never needed Him this desperately before.

My husband Marty made a commitment not to read the newspaper that first year of her illness, and instead spent more time reading the miracle stories of Jesus and writing out healing scriptures. We compiled pages of scriptures that told us God truly is a healing, delivering God. But we would get discouraged as we watched Anna Joy unable to move around like other children, so we began looking for present day stories of miracles. We watched videos and read testimonies of healings. Those stories encouraged us that nothing was impossible with God. We believed that what He had done for others, He could do for us.

As we got stronger in our faith that God was truly a healing God, we treated Anna Joy like she was healed as much as possible. It was a process. But as we focused on the truth in Scripture, God strengthened our faith until it became a part of us. It was not just someone else's teaching or belief; it was in our hearts so much that we almost wanted to scream out to anyone who would listen, "God is a healing God!" As a family, we began declaring God's healing over Anna Joy no matter what the circumstances looked like in the natural or how foolish we looked. They weren't empty words, but came from our deep faith and belief that God could do it. We absolutely believed God would heal Anna Joy based on our understanding that Jesus spent so much of His life on earth healing people; and He is the same yesterday, today and forever.

Most importantly during this time, we fell more in love with Jesus and His Word. We trusted Him no matter what, even if He didn't heal our daughter. We loved Him and believed He was powerful, that He cared about our situation, and that He still healed even if we didn't see our healing. Every day for months we would talk to Anna Joy as if she could hear us, believing at any moment she would start kicking her feet, sitting up, and crawling—something to manifest the healing we believed so strongly in our hearts.

Then one day she tracked with her eyes, following me. She seemed to respond to the sound of my voice. Progressively from twelve months to eighteen months Anna Joy was completely restored. Medical science said it was impossible, but God's Word says that nothing is impossible to those who believe.

Her head had been enlarged, and she had not shown the growth of a normal child, but at twelve months, she began changing. I remember the day the nurse told me very excitedly that they began charting her growth on normal charts! Her eyesight and motor skills became completely normal. Her hearing was restored except for in one ear, but it does not impair her in any way. I believe that is to remind her of what an awesome healing God has done for her. I had been telling the MHMR people that we would not need them for long. We rejoiced when they finally agreed.

God has truly done a modern miracle. To see Anna Joy now you would never know she should have been retarded and crippled. She is an A/B student, and participates in all the sports and activities any child would. We truly know God still heals and delivers people today!

We pray that as you read the rest of this book, you will be inspired to believe God for the impossible. God is moving in unprecedented ways all over the earth to heal, deliver, and reveal Himself to people. If you or anyone you know needs healing or deliverance from pain and addictions, we believe that you will be touched as you read these pages, and that you will not only get your miracle, but also help others get theirs. If you are a believer and you have let go of believing God for the miraculous, we encourage you to once again pray for God to touch your life and the lives around you in powerful ways. God wants to show Himself in His glory through you.

CHAPTER 1

Laying a Foundation

I did not have the privilege of knowing very much about God growing up. I did not grow up in church or know any Bible stories. When I was ten, my babysitter asked me if I knew what a Christian was, and I said, "No." She simply explained that a Christian was someone who believed that Jesus was God's Son, and that He came to earth to die on the cross for the sins of everyone who would accept His forgiveness. She said that if I asked God to forgive me of my sins and asked Jesus to come into my life, He would, and I would never be separated from Him; even when I died, I would go to heaven to be with Him. I prayed with her that day and I knew from then on that I was a Christian.

As a college student, I remember not knowing the difference between Easter and Christmas: which one was celebrating Jesus' birth and which one was about His death and resurrection. I did not know the simplest truths from God's Word. I met some sincere, strong Christians in college. I loved what I saw in them, but my lifestyle was so far from theirs. I didn't know how to change or be like them. A few weeks later, I had a car accident and ran into a metal blockade that read "Dead End." I felt these words deep in my heart: "You are going into a dead end road. Turn completely to Me and follow Me." I knew it was God. I was gripped by such a strong presence of God. I remember crying and crying, knowing my life would never be the same.

From that day on, my life dramatically changed. I hungered for God, wanted to go to church, read the Bible, and found Christian friends. I easily ended all destructive relationships in my life almost overnight.

During those beginning years of growing as a Christian, I believed everything I read in the Bible. When I read about Jesus healing, I just knew that was the kind, sweet Jesus I was getting to know. I found it easy to ask Him for healing when I or someone I knew needed it. When I heard of miracles in the Bible or a supernatural story a missionary told, I believed it. Over the years, I have found that many people are skeptical and unbelieving of miracle stories, which greatly affects their ability to believe that God would help them in a supernatural way when they are in great need.

I want to distinguish between immediate healings obtained through the ministry of those with supernatural gifts, and healings obtained through a process of exercising faith and standing on God's Word alone. Even people who may believe that God is powerful enough to heal them, but don't expect Him to really do it, can receive immediate healing when someone with the gift of healing prays for them. God pours out His mercy, and these miracles happen, which I thank Him for. However, it is not God's only way, or even His primary way of healing His people. We cannot control this kind of healing, or make it happen. The gifts of healing or miracles are given out as the Spirit wills, as 1 Corinthians 12:11 says. More often, God heals when it's taught that He's a healing God, and people believe His Word, pray for the sick, and yield to the Holy Spirit.

When we found out about Anna Joy's prognosis, we were immediately frightened. We knew God was our only help. We looked up all the healing scriptures we could find and depended on God. We called our pastor right away because he is a man of faith, but our main dependence was on Jesus. We went to several healing services, but our emphasis was on God, His Word and what He promised us. We knew we could depend on God's faithfulness to His Word even if a sudden miracle did not easily come.

God wants each of us to establish our own faith in His Word no matter what challenging circumstances come our way. We can build our lives on the Word of God and develop a strong trust in Him. We are not left waiting for only one option—a person with the gift of healing or miracles when the difficult trials come our way. God has given us His Word and His Holy Spirit, which are available 365 days a year, 24 hours a day. It is important to know what God teaches in His Word about healing and to know that you or I can pray for ourselves, our friends, spouse or kids even in the middle of the night for healing and God will answer.

One night when I went to bed, the tip of my tongue was hurting like it does when you burn it on soup or hot chocolate. It had hurt for a couple of days, but I figured it was just a little burned, although I did not recall burning it. I figured it would go away shortly. That evening my tongue kept hurting and now it was swelling. I woke my husband and said, "Marty, my tongue is beginning to swell and it hurts." He said, "The Bible says that by His stripes you are healed! You're healed - go to bed!" He never even rolled over to look at me. A little later, I woke him up again, this time with my tongue literally hanging out of my mouth. He responded the same way two more times, never looking at me. I knew in my spirit man that he was right, but my tongue still hurt.

I got up out of bed finally about 4:00 AM and began reading the pages of stapled healing scriptures we had written out during Anna Joy's sickness. I read them over and over, even saying some out loud. After a while, I turned on the TV. Since it was a Sunday morning, I began watching one of my favorite Bible teachers that also teaches on healing. All of a sudden, I understood a dream I had had a few nights before. The dream had not made any sense to me until that moment.

In the dream, I wanted to buy a house that we did not qualify for. I nervously went to an office to apply for the financing, and I was aware that I had altered my identification. I had taped a picture of Jesus over my picture like a fake I.D. I knew it was probably not going to pass. In my dream, I handed it to a mean-looking man at the counter and said, "I want to apply for money for a house. " He said, "NO, you do not qualify." I said very nervously, "I appeal to *Him*," pointing to a Man behind the mean man who had His back to me. As this Man turned to look at me, I could see it was Jesus. He said, "Give her whatever she says." I knew by His Word and authority that I had received what I needed, and that the mean man could not keep it from me.

Immediately the interpretation of the dream was clear to me. I did not qualify for any of God's promises on my own; I could not earn them or be good enough. My salvation, my needs for peace, provision, healing, etc. would only be met because of Jesus' payment for them on the cross. He gave me His identity and He qualified me. He stamps His identity right over mine. Therefore I can ask for whatever I need, and the enemy cannot stop it. Jesus said in the dream, "Give her whatever she <u>says</u>." I believe that is often where we miss it as believers. Jesus paid for it, He has provided it, and we may believe it in our hearts, but faith is released through our words and actions. Remember, James 2:17 says, "...faith by itself, if it is not accompanied by action, is dead." (NIV) We fail to ask boldly or speak in faith before we receive something.

We think too naturally, and want to see to believe, when God's way is to believe and then see.

As soon as I realized the meaning of the dream, my tongue immediately went back to normal. It was amazing! I have never forgotten that experience. Many scriptures confirm that the Holy Spirit speaks to us through dreams. To find out if a dream is from the Holy Spirit and not just the pizza you ate the night before, see if it agrees with the Word of God. Always go with the Word over experience, but thank God for such experiences that clarify His Word.

To see and receive healing, we must develop a strong foundation on God's Word. In this study, we will help build this foundation and gain understanding of what faith is, how to appropriate it, and ultimately, how to stand until our manifestation comes! We will feed on the Word of God, believe it, and act upon it!

My challenge to you is to be a doer of the Word; pray for the sick and leave the results to Him. If you are afraid of disappointing people, just love them sensitively, gently, and simply, without being strange. They will feel more loved by Jesus than before you prayed for them, and you can count on Him finishing the work. Jesus was always moved with compassion, and when people are hurting and sick, they need us to show them the compassion and love of Jesus. But always give God the opportunity to heal by obeying His Word and praying for the sick.

CHAPTER 2

Establishing the Word of God as Truth

"All scripture is inspired by God and profitable for teaching, for reproof, for correction, for training in righteousness." II Timothy 3:16

We must first establish in our hearts that the Bible is true. The Bible is the final authority. The Amplified version of the verse above says, "Every scripture is God-breathed—given by His inspiration—and profitable for instruction, for reproof and conviction of <u>sin</u>, <u>for correction</u> of <u>error</u> and discipline in obedience, and for training in righteousness."

When Billy Graham was beginning his ministry, he had a friend that traveled with him. They both were trained at the same Bible school and preached together. One day, the friend started doubting the Word of God and saying it did not mean what it said; he started backing off the scriptures and making up his own philosophies. Billy Graham went out to the woods by an old stump and cried out to God for truth. Finally, he set his Bible down on the ground, stood on it, and declared out loud for all of heaven to hear that he was going to believe the absolute authority of God's Word, and not doubt it. He would give his life to teach it as truth, no matter what the philosophy of man said. The story goes that the other man spent the rest of his life as an atheist. When asked about Jesus right before he died, he said, "I miss Him."

To have faith in God's Word, we, too, have to make a firm decision that His Word is the final authority. We have to make up our minds about what we believe the Bible is. Some see the Bible as no more than a history book, or as a "religious book only scholars can interpret." I believe it is our manual for life; God's Word to us. It is to be trusted for our instruction, encouragement and inspiration for life. When we are at odds with it, it is still the final authority, and we must yield to it and not try to change it to conform to our wants or desires.

I believe the best way to study the Bible is to lay down all preconceived ideas and then purpose to obey God's truth and instructions. Traditionally in the church, as we have learned the Bible, we have emphasized certain portions while remaining unaware of powerful truths also contained in the scriptures. For example, Psalm 103:2-3 says, **"Praise the Lord, O my soul, and forget not all His benefits—Who forgives all your sins and heals all your diseases."** This scripture says that just as God has forgiven us, He has healed us. Because the forgiveness of sin is what is most often preached, we miss the equally important point that God heals our diseases. We need to agree with all of what the Word of God says instead of just what tradition emphasizes.

Second Timothy 3:16 says, "All scripture is God-breathed and is useful for teaching, rebuking, correcting, and training in righteousness..." If we genuinely submit our minds and understanding to God, He will correct any error we have. Philippians 3:15 states, "If we are otherwise minded, God shall reveal even this to us."

A friend who is a physician struggled with severe migraines for years. He and his wife love people. They are constantly opening their home to alcohol and drug addicts, sharing the love of Jesus and praying for their healing and deliverance. One evening my friend went out to a field to pray and got really honest with God. He told the Lord he believed he was healed according to the Word, but had not experienced it for himself. He needed to know for himself that God truly heals today.

He read afresh all the healing scriptures he knew and cried out to God for his own healing. God healed my friend, and now he treats people medically and also prays for their supernatural healing in a very sincere way.

Let's pray: *Dear Lord, I purpose to set aside any error I believe about You, Your Word, and Your healing power. Purge my heart and mind of any false understanding and unbelief. And, Holy Spirit, teach me truth from God's Word. In Jesus' Name, Amen.*

Throughout the Old Testament, God declares that if He speaks a matter, it is established, dependable, and reliable for us to live by. I Kings 8:56b says, **"...not one word has failed of all the wonderful promises He gave through His servant Moses."** If God says something, it will not fail. The Bible is an entire book of God speaking to us.

Psalm 119:89 states, **"Forever, O Lord, Your Word stands firm in heaven."** Not only is God's Word established when He speaks it, but He will move whatever He has to in order to make sure it happens. Jeremiah 1:12 says, **"...for I will hasten My Word to perform it."**

Sometimes people give us their word on something, but fail to fulfill it for various reasons. It is very common for us to have tremendous doubt and even fear in regards to taking the Bible for what it actually says. But when God says something, He means it! God's Word, the Bible, is filled with Him talking to us. He is telling us His promises to mankind, and He will fulfill what He says. In Numbers 23:19 we find, **"God is not a man that He should lie; He is not a human, that He should change his mind. Has He ever spoken and failed to act? Has He ever promised and not carried it through?"**

Joshua 21:45 restates this: **"All of the good promises that the Lord has given Israel came true."**

We inherit salvation by believing and confessing the Word of God. As Romans 10:9 says, "If you confess with your mouth Jesus is Lord and believe in your heart God raised him from the dead you will be saved." It doesn't depend on our feelings.

Psalm 37:23 says, "The steps of a righteous man are ordered by the Lord." This brings me great comfort when I'm not sure what to do. I believe God's Word and say to myself, "I'm surrendered to God and His will for my life, therefore, God, You will order my steps." There is a trust in His Word to lead me.

I know there are always people around that tell you, "The Bible doesn't mean that," or, "Those Old Testament scriptures are not for us." Anna Joy is living proof that it is God's will to heal today. There were lots of people telling us not to get our hopes up, that sometimes God does not heal. Some would even say, "You are putting a demand on God and you shouldn't do that."

We simply believed the Bible just the way it was written. We focused on God being true to His Word, despite how Anna Joy looked or how the tests came back. We knew she was in serious trouble, but we believed the supernatural power of God and His Word— that God was a God who could change the natural circumstances in Anna Joy's life if we believed.

To live victoriously, we need to know that the Bible is God speaking to us through the Holy Spirit. When we take His Word personally and believe it, it energizes us and gives life to our bodies.

In I Thessalonians 2:13 we read, **"And for this reason we also constantly thank God that when you received from us the <u>Word of God's</u> message, you accepted it not as the word of men, but for what it really is, the <u>Word of God</u>, which also performs its work in you who**

believe." When I read this, I would say to myself, "This is God speaking to me. God's Word will perform all that I need. It is healing to Anna Joy's body. I believe it. It is the Word of God and not the word of men."

I remember when I was coming out of a compromising and sinful lifestyle as a college student. I wanted to walk with God, but my choices were still contradictory to a holy life. Jeremiah 23:29 says that the **Word of God is like fire**. After being out doing things I should not do, I would get my Bible and write out scriptures like, "Be holy for I am holy." My mind would say, "You're not holy," but I would read and write out the scripture over and over and say to myself, "I am holy. God says I am. He has made me holy." It's been twenty-five years since then that I've lived holy, and I believe God will keep me holy until I meet Him in heaven. The Word of God is like fire that will separate any harmful way from us and help us walk in peace, love, and victory.

My husband has asked me for years whenever I've faced a challenge, "What scripture do you have on that problem?" Sometimes I wanted to whine and talk about the problem and he would push me to ask, "What does God say about that?" This forced me to make a decision to walk by faith, to look up what God has done in His Word for someone else and say, "He can do that for me." An opportunity to practice this principle came when I was interviewing for a pharmaceutical position. I had been a stay-at-home mom for ten years, and now I had to study and take many tests. As I was driving to Dallas to take the final test, fear tried to grip my heart. I had to yield to peace and say Proverbs 10:7, "'The memory of the just is blessed.' I will remember what I have studied. I have God's favor and I will pass this test." I was thinking seriously of turning around and going home because of the fear. God helped me and I passed. It was a blessing. The Word of God will strengthen us in whatever we face.

One of my favorite Old Testament stories is that of the widow who had sold all she had to pay her debt, but she still didn't have enough. The debt collectors were coming to take her children as slaves to pay back the rest. She cried out to the prophet of God, and he instructed her to get the only thing she had left in her house, a jar of oil, and to pour that oil into as many borrowed jars as she could. When she did this, a miracle happened! The oil kept coming and filling more and more jars. She sold them, and made enough money to pay all her debt and live on the rest (II Kings 4)!

When I read stories like this one, I think, "Wow, Look at God! He can cancel debt in a day. If He did it for that widow He can do it for us." There was a time when my husband and I were in a serious amount of debt and just couldn't seem to get ahead. We would pray and remind God, "You are a supernatural God; You can cancel our debt in a day. We believe that You are not a respecter of persons; what You've done for others, You'll do for us. You will cause us to be debt free and a blessing to people financially!" It took all the faith we could muster when bills were overdue; even buying diapers and groceries was difficult during those days. One couple I know experienced their huge school debt getting cancelled in a day, but for us it was a process of listening to God and making changes vocationally. He led us bit by bit, and how sweet it is now to be free of debt and to be able to support several missionaries, to be a blessing instead of always needing that financial miracle. The way God does it or His timing may not be our way, but He is faithful to provide for us.

Another couple I'm aware of had been trying to travel and sing while making music CD's and had accumulated tremendous debt. Leaders of a larger ministry had dinner with them and in one evening, paid all their debt and booked them for the next year. That seems just like the story from the Bible, doesn't it? You cannot separate God's Word from Himself, as seen in John 1:1-2—"In the beginning was the Word, and the Word was with God, and the Word was God." The Word was God. (v.2) "He (the Word) was in the beginning with God." John 1:14—"And the Word became flesh, and dwelt among us..." Revelation 19:13—"And He is clothed with a robe dipped in blood; and His name is called the Word of God."

Strong's *Exhaustive Concordance of the Bible* says that when "word" is used in the Old Testament, it means "as matter spoken of; word; advice; spoken; talk." Strong's gives the definition of "word" in the New Testament as "something said; Divine expression; utterance; word." Through these similar definitions, we see that God's Word is just as dependable in the Old Testament as it is in the New Testament. God's written Word is His Divine expression, so we can conclude it is His will for us. Thus, the scriptures we read should be taken personally as God speaking to us.

Vine's *Expository Dictionary of New Testament Words* gives similar definitions to Strong's *Concordance*, but adds that "word" denotes a "message from the Lord, delivered with His authority and made effective by His power." Wow! God's Word is His will! It contains His authority and power to perform what is needed.

Today, there are popular movies and other media that try to get people to distrust the Word of God. As Christians, we need to be solid in our trust of Jesus, of God and His Word, because they are one. Jesus told us that everything He did and said was His Father's will. So we can be confident that each healing Jesus did was God's will. Every scripture is what God is speaking and is His will for us.

I remember taking several religion classes when I was in college. One professor said that all stories recorded before Moses in the Bible were Jewish fables that never really happened. Another professor explained away every miracle in the New Testament. I decided then that I believed the Bible and not man's philosophies. I am glad I made that decision, because Anna Joy is well today.

It is important for you to make a determination that God's Word is true, and that you will believe what it says concerning your life and health today. God's Word is our manual for life. It will instruct us how to pick a godly mate, raise our kids, and live with integrity and holiness. To live closely with the Lord and victoriously, we have to order our lives by God's Word and His Spirit. For example, if a single woman is interested in marrying an unbeliever, she is being disobedient to the Word of God. The Bible says not to be yoked to an unbeliever. If a married man decides he is tired of his wife and desires his friend's mate, he is committing adultery in his heart. It is surprising how many times people say, "God said that it was okay." No, God did not say that! God will not contradict his Word. We need to be a people of integrity with God's way of living. I can tell you, it is the sweetest life ever to walk with Jesus in obedience to His Word.

CHAPTER 3

Healing Belongs to Believers

Now that we have established in our hearts that whatever God's Word says is true, trustworthy, and dependable, let's see if God's Word provides healing.

In the Old Testament there are seven redemptive names of Jehovah. Jehovah means, "The self-existent One Who reveals Himself" (*Strong's Concordance*). Redemption means, "to rescue; ransom; salvation." God's names tell us about His nature; He embodies these redemptive names to us.

1. Jehovah-Shammah "The Lord is there or present." **("I will never leave you or forsake you." Hebrews 13:5)**

2. Jehovah-Shalom "The Lord, our peace." **(Jesus said, "My peace I give unto you." John 14:27)**

3. Jehovah-Ra-ah "The Lord, my shepherd." **(Psalm 23:1)**

4. Jehovah-Jireh "The Lord will provide." **("And my God will supply all your needs according to His riches in glory in Christ Jesus." Philippians 4:19)**

5. Jehovah-Nissi "The Lord is our banner." **("Thanks be to God which gives us the victory through**

our Lord Jesus Christ." I
Corinthians 15:57)

6. Jehovah-Tsidkenu "The Lord, our righteousness."
**("For He has made Him to be
sin for us, who knew no sin;
that we might be made the
righteousness of God in Him."
II Corinthians 5:21)**

7. Jehovah-Rapha "The Lord, our healer."
**("I am the Lord who heals
you." Exodus 15:26)**

From the beginning of time until now, none of these
names of God have changed. He is who He says He is.
He is our present help, our peace, our shepherd, our
provider, our banner, our righteousness. And <u>He is the
Lord, OUR HEALER!</u> That is good news!

One of my favorite healing stories is about a lady
named Betty Baxter. As a child she had tumors all
down her spine, and she could not lift her head. During
the day, her mother would lay her in a chair. She was
so bent over and small for her age that her younger
brother called her "little sis." Until one day...sweet
Jesus spoke to her heart that He was going to heal her.
God spoke to her mother during the same time. Her
mother had been praying for Betty's healing most of
her life, but hearing Jesus speak to her directly about
it encouraged her. Over the next months Betty grew
worse. When she was near death, her father came in
and picked her up. He told her how much he loved
her, and how he had spent everything he had at the
best hospitals to try to heal her, but soon she would be
going to heaven. With tears he said his goodbyes. But

her mother called friends in to pray for Betty's healing. While they were praying, Betty had a vision of a willow tree bent over. Jesus walked over to it and straightened it up. In the same vision, Jesus walked over to Betty and touched her tummy and all her internal organs went into place. Then He touched her spine. Everyone heard popping as each vertebra went into place, and she stood up completely healed. Betty Baxter's healing is a marvelous story of something impossible in the natural becoming possible through the miraculous and supernatural. Exodus 15:26 says, "I am the Lord who heals you"—Jehovah Rapha! God would not give us His name as Healer without backing it up. When we call on Jehovah Rapha, the Lord our Physician is there to heal us even when it looks impossible.

God's Word says in Exodus 23:25-26, "I will bless your food and water and I will take sickness away from the midst of you." My father-in-law prays this scripture at every meal.

My mother-in-law's doctor convinced her to have a mammogram since her mother had died of cancer in her early forties. It showed lots of fibroid cysts, so they called her for more tests. The doctors were very concerned and scheduled a specialist for the next day. My mother-in-law is a woman who prays daily and believes the Word of God. She and her husband prayed and believed God for a good report, and the following day the same tests showed absolutely nothing. It totally baffled the radiologist! My in-laws knew they could confidently pray God's Word to Him and He would move on their behalf. They didn't waver thinking, "Will God help us or not?" They believed the scriptures, and spoke them back to God even when circumstances were contrary to what they were praying. They prayed, "God, Your Word says that You remove sickness and disease away from us, and we believe it." They prayed the Word instead of the problem.

My in-laws have not always walked with God. It wasn't until their late forties that they asked Jesus to be the Lord of their lives. But when they started learning the Word of God, it began to change their lives. Most of their kids were on drugs at the time (my mother-in-law had eight children and my father-in-law had seven when they married, and they had one together), and their house was full of rebellion, cussing, and strife. As they surrendered to Jesus and got up daily to pray and read the Bible, over time their home became a house of peace. Now, almost all their children are walking with the Lord strongly, and many are in the ministry.

God can bring order, and emotional as well as physical healing. He desires that our home be a house of refuge and godly living. He can show us how. There are so many things that pull our families into destructive addictions and illnesses. We need the power of God in our homes. He wants to be there to bring victory and abundant life to us. Rebellion, pornography, and sicknesses do not come from God. He is good and wants His people blessed. Sin and sickness are in the world because of Satan. Deuteronomy 28:1 states that if we will obey the voice of the Lord and do His commands, then His blessings will come upon us and overtake us.

Say out loud right now, *"Lord, Your Word says You are Jehovah Rapha, the God who heals me. I believe You are who You say You are, my Healer. I receive Your healing now in my mind, my body, my emotions and my relationships. I ask for Your presence and peace in my home. Thank You, Lord."*

God wants a relationship with us. He wants to be involved in our daily lives, and He wants us to follow

His ways and be overshadowed with His blessings. However, in Deuteronomy 28:15, He tells us, "But if you refuse to listen to the Lord your God and do not obey all the commands and laws I am giving you today, all these curses will come and overwhelm you." In verses 21-61, God proceeds to list these curses. At the end, in verse 61, He says that, "all sicknesses, and every plague which is not written in the book of the law," will come upon the people if they are disobedient. This clearly states that sicknesses are a result of a curse.

In these passages, God is stating that blessings come from obedience, and curses from disobedience. Sickness is not listed with the blessings. That is not to say that if you are sick there is definitely a place of disobedience in your life. The devil and his curses are active in the world because of the fall of man. There are hereditary diseases, harmful chemicals in the environment, and poor nutrition, along with many other reasons for diseases. But nothing is impossible with God. Whether your sickness is a result of disobedience, such as a disease contracted through drug abuse or immorality, or not, Jesus has provided a way out.

The good news is that Jesus redeemed us from the curses. Galatians 3:13 says, **"Christ has redeemed us from the curse of the law, having become a curse for us (for it is written, "Cursed is everyone who hangs on a tree")** (NKJV). Until Satan is bound, sickness and poverty will continue on the earth, but Jesus came to take the curse of eternal death and sickness away from us so we can be free from them. Just as we receive eternal salvation by believing the Word of God, we receive healing by faith in the Word of God.

I remember that when Anna Joy was sick, my husband asked what he did wrong to have this come upon our child. My father-in-law wisely said, "The correct question is *what to do now*?" I think questions like "Why has this happened?" "Why has God allowed this?" or "Why, if God is good and I am His child, is this happening?" are all crippling. Jesus said that in this life we would have trouble.

There is a place of being honest with God and repentant if we have sinned. We need to have our slates clean with Him when we go to Him for our needs. I John 1:9 says, **"If we confess our sins, He is faithful and just to forgive us."** According to God's Word, Jesus paid for our sins no matter how horrible they are, and if we truly confess them and receive Jesus in our lives, He will wipe our slate clean. He puts our sin in the pit of forgetfulness.

No matter what the reason for the affliction, whether it's sickness, rebellious children, addiction, a difficult marriage, or imprisonment, God has provided a way for healing and wholeness. That doesn't mean deliverance is always automatic; sometimes it is a process, especially when relationships have been damaged. Bodies need to be strengthened and new habits need to be formed in order for full transformation to happen. Unfortunately, for many years the enemy has blinded believers from seeing that just as Jesus paid for our forgiveness, He also took our sickness, weakness, and pain, as Isaiah 53 declares.

Much of Jesus' ministry was healing and deliverance, which clearly illustrates God's heart to override natural law and to heal us when we are sick and deliver us when we are in bondage. The early church understood this: the scriptures show the apostles healing the sick. Somehow, the modern church has only heard the salvation message of eternity with Jesus. So when we teach healing as part of the New Covenant, our minds need much renewing in order to believe. It may be that many of us have not experienced very much healing, and unbelief is the prevalent thought. I want my mind renewed by the Word of God, and for us to be the church of the Bible, not of current teaching and experiences.

In Matthew 7:24-27 Jesus taught a story about a wise man who built his house on a rock. He said that the rain came, the streams rose, the winds blew and beat against that house, yet it did not fall. The reason it did not fall is seen in verse 24: <u>He listened to Jesus' words and put them into practice</u>. This man was a hearer and a doer of the Word. Jesus contrasts this story with that of the foolish man whose house fell. The foolish man <u>heard the word and did not do what it said</u>. The storms came against both houses, but Jesus told us how to keep our house standing anyway: hear the Word and do it!

God tells us, "The storms will come; many are the afflictions of the righteous, but the Lord will deliver us out of them all." Remember the ending of this verse: **"He will deliver us out of them all"** (Psalm 34:19).

My position is to keep my eyes on Jesus. He says He is the author and perfecter of my faith. Once I have asked the Holy Spirit to search my heart and have confessed my sin, I let it go and refuse to get bogged down in the "why's." I think they are robbers of trust and faith in God's goodness. My answer to "why" is, "I trust Him." I am going to concentrate on what He tells me to do instead of questioning Him and looking back.

John 16:33 (AMP) says, **"I have told you these things, so that in Me you may have (perfect) peace and confidence. In the world you have tribulation and trials and distress and frustration; but be of good cheer (take courage; be confident, certain, undaunted) for I have**

overcome the world. (I have deprived it of power to harm you and have conquered it for you.)" We should not be surprised when trials come our way, but we must decide what we will do with them. Will we wallow in self-pity, blame God, take whatever the devil or life throws at us without a fight? Or will we grab hold of God and say, "God, You are good. You are faithful, and my hope is in none other than You. Lead me, show me if there are natural means like diet changes or medicine. Help me, Lord, to fight the fight of faith and watch Your wonderful deliverance come to pass in my life. Show me how to walk strong and overcome through this trial."

As I said before, when Anna Joy was diagnosed, we did all that was possible medically yet also ran to God, believing He could and would heal her. My husband and I never had a conversation that doubted it, nor asked, "What will we do if she isn't healed?" I knew that regardless of her healing, God was still good. In the back of my mind, I determined that I would always walk as close to Him as I could. I would still believe that He is in the business of healing no matter what our outcome was. I based my life on His Word and not on my experience, and determined that I would continue to pray for the healing of others. We have people who are in the middle of physical problems on our healing team at church. God uses them, and many people are healed through their prayers even though they haven't seen their own breakthrough yet.

The story of Shadrach, Meshach and Abednego told in Daniel 3 encourages me in this. These Hebrews refused to bow to King Nebuchadnezzar's idol. The king got mad and threw them in a fiery furnace. Before they entered the furnace, they said, **"Our God will deliver us, oh king, but if not, let it be known that we will not**

bow." I have thought a lot about that story and I agree with their statement. In faith, based on God's Word the best I know, my God will heal Anna Joy. ***But if not***, I still believe He is Jehovah Rapha: He loves us; He heals us; He answers us when we cry out to Him. Even when Anna Joy was sick, we passed out hundreds of stapled healing scriptures to anyone who wanted them. We gave out books and tapes on healing, because our hearts were full of the goodness of God no matter what the turnout was for us. There were lots of incredible healing testimonies out there and our faith was stirred when we would hear them. We wanted to share His goodness with people to remind ourselves and others what a big God we have.

Say out loud: *"Lord, You are trustworthy. You are good in all Your ways. I may not understand everything right now, but I know You are good. I know You answer prayer. I know I may be afflicted now, but Your Word says You will deliver me out of them all. You are my deliverer, my healer, my provider. Your hand is not short that it cannot save me. I believe You will save, heal, and deliver me from all my affliction."*

Let's look at Isaiah 53:4-5. It is a very important passage to study in regard to healing and all that Jesus came to pay for on the cross. It says, **"Surely He hath borne our griefs (Hebrew-sicknesses) and carried our sorrows (Hebrew-diseases): yet we did esteem Him stricken, smitten of God, and afflicted. But He was wounded for our transgressions, He was bruised for our iniquities: the chastisement of our peace was upon Him; and with His stripes we are healed."** (KJV)

We do not use the term "borne" today. It means to lift up, to bear away. Jesus bore away our sicknesses and carried off our diseases. In Leviticus 16:22, we learn about an Old Testament religious practice that the priests performed every year in which they symbolically placed the sins of the people on a goat. The sins were put on the goat by faith in obedience to God's command. The goat bore the sins of the people as it was sent away, symbolizing the taking away of their sins for one year.

The good news about Jesus is that He took all of our sins and bore them away forever, not only for a year. He took all past, present, and future sins on the cross. All the sicknesses of the world were put on Jesus at the cross. He took our grief, sorrow, and depression; mental and emotional healing has been purchased for you by Jesus. He took them upon Himself so that we, by faith, might believe and receive forgiveness of sins and healing. That is why I Peter 2:24 says, **"By his stripes we were healed."** We are not asking God to do something new.

Notice that in the above Isaiah 53 passage, it says, **"The chastisement of our peace was upon Him."** My mother suffered for many years from mental and emotional problems. When she was fifty, she had a hallucination in which she thought my stepfather was trying to kill her. She asked me to check the attic for bombs. I knew she was not thinking clearly, but I appeased her. As I reported to her from the attic that everything looked fine, I turned and fell through the sheet rock, catching my arms on the beams while a nail went through one underarm. Even though I was bleeding and in tremendous pain, and my mother was screaming beneath me, a supernatural peace came over me. I instructed my mother to get the ladder and take me to the hospital. The first report wasn't good. The doctors thought that my arms were broken, and that they would have to call in a specialist to stitch up the muscle the nail went through.

I was in college at the time, and had just been to a healing seminar. When they put me in the x-ray room, I prayed over my arms, just as I'd seen the week before at the seminar. I prayed the only healing scripture I knew at the time, "By his stripes I am healed" (I Peter 2:24). I asked God to heal me, and He did at that very moment. I don't even remember being sore the next day. The best news is that the supernatural peace God showered on me during that time led my mom to ask Jesus to take over her life that night. She said, "I want that peace that only Jesus could bring." Over time, God completely healed my mom. My mom is living proof of complete emotional healing. She has so much life now, and vivaciously shares the love of God. She is an amazing grandmother, mother, and friend. You would never know she struggled in her emotions those years before. That is Amazing Grace.

Since my mother's salvation, my stepfather has given his life to Jesus also. They led my grandparents, aunts, uncles, and cousins to Jesus. One cousin was agoraphobic. He lived with his parents and had not left the house in eight years, and only would come out of his room to the kitchen. He discovered Jesus and was completely healed. He eventually moved out and married a believer. We have seen so many miracles of God in the lives of our family and friends. There is nothing too difficult for God.

1 Peter 2:24 refers directly to the Isaiah 53 passage. It is one of many New Testament references to Jesus' payment on the cross for our sins and sicknesses. It says of Jesus that ***"He personally bore our sins in His own body on the tree that we might die to sin and live to righteousness; by whose stripes we were healed."***

Since the first edition of Anna Joy's story, we've received great testimonies from readers. One was of a young man who was hopelessly addicted to drugs and alcohol. At the time he came to see his mother, he was completely discouraged about getting free of the addictions that were killing him. His mom had just read our book and told him he could read it; it was a story of how God did the impossible. Much to her surprise, he sat down and read the book and did not get off the couch until he finished. God, in His great love and mercy, touched him and delivered him from all his addictions. He found a church and Christian friends and he has totally been changed. I had the privilege of going to his church to minister not long ago, and he came up to speak with me. He introduced me to his wife and told me how he has been free for several years and serves faithfully in his church. What a delivering God we have!

In Matthew 8:16-17, we read that Jesus healed all who came to Him. We see Isaiah 53 again in this passage: **"When evening had come, they brought to Him many who were demon-possessed. And He cast out the spirits with a word, and healed all who were sick, that it might be fulfilled which was spoken by Isaiah the prophet, saying: "He Himself took our infirmities and bore our sicknesses."** (NKJV) Jesus died for our sin and sicknesses, **"Who, His own self, bore our sins in His body on the tree, that we, being dead to sins, should live unto righteousness: by whose stripes we were healed"** (I Peter 2:24).

If you had an insurance policy but did not know your benefits, you could spend a lot of money unnecessarily on things already covered. But if you were aware of your benefits, you could be saved the expenses the insurance was created to cover. The same is true with God. You can miss out on His best by not knowing your benefits. He tells us not to forget His benefits: **"Praise the**

Lord, O my soul, and forget not all His benefits—who forgives all our sins and who heals all your diseases." (Psalm 103:2-3) Don't neglect this wonderful benefit of healing that God has provided.

Proverbs 4:22 says, **"God's promises are life to those that find them, and health to all their flesh."** If you go through your life without finding His promises, you may miss the health He has provided. A certain pastor's wife at our church has a wonderful deliverance story. When she was around ten, she suffered a complete mental and emotional breakdown. She regressed so much that she lost her ability to read, write, or do math assignments. She was released from school and sent to a psychiatrist who said she would never recover. She was put on strong medications for the many seizures she was having. But her mother would not accept that her daughter would always be in that condition. She began praying over her diligently and insisted that they put her back in school. There is power in a mama's prayers. The school put her in the special education program, but within a year she was completely delivered. She was moved into the regular classroom once again, and she graduated from high school with honors. My friend became quite a woman of faith. She went to a Christian college with no money, taking each step by faith and seeing God provide for her needs. Years later, she had a newborn daughter that almost died, but because she had seen God do the supernatural and knew how to pray and believe God, her daughter was healed and another testimony won.

The things we overcome become powerful anchors for our lives. That is why the devil fights us so much. Once we have seen God do the impossible for us, we know personally that He will walk with us and help us no matter what comes at us in life. 1 Peter 5:8 TLB says,

"Be careful, watch out for attacks from Satan, your great enemy. He prowls around like a hungry, roaring lion, looking for some victim to tear apart. Stand firm when he attacks. Trust the Lord... After you have suffered a little while, our God personally will come and pick you up, and set you firmly in place and make you stronger than ever."

More promises of healing:

Psalm 107:20 **"God sent His Word and healed them."** *His Word is health to us.*

Jeremiah 17:14 **"Heal me, O Lord, and I shall be healed; save me, and I shall be saved; my praises are for You alone."**

Jeremiah 30:17 **"For I will give you back your health and heal your wounds says the Lord."**

Say out loud: *"God, Your Word is health to all my flesh. I am reading and meditating on Your Word and it brings my body healing. It is alive and active, and Your power will perform Your Word. Thank You for taking the stripes on Your back for my healing. I receive the health You paid for right now! Thank You for the many testimonies of healing You are doing around the world. Do Your mighty works in my world, God. I ask You to move unhindered in Your mighty power in my life and in my family and friends."*

CHAPTER 4

The Life and Ministry of Jesus as Healer

When I think of the life of Jesus, I can't help but think of how much time He spent healing people. Hebrews 1:3 says, "The Son is the radiance of God's glory and the exact representation of His being." To me this says that Jesus is the exact representation of God. It gives the picture that what we see Jesus doing and saying is exactly what God wants. When Jesus heals, God is saying, "I want you well." The sweet life of Jesus with His compassion for hurting people is God's heart. It hasn't changed. If Jesus were here in the flesh today, He would spend a lot of time healing hurting, sick people.

First, let's look at the multitudes Jesus healed:

1) "And Jesus went about all Galilee, teaching... and preaching the Gospel...and healing all manner of disease among the people. And His fame went throughout all Syria; and they brought unto Him all sick people that were taken with various diseases and pains, demoniacs, epileptics, paralytics; and He healed them all." (Matthew 4:23-24)

2) "And Jesus went about all the cities and villages teaching...and healing every kind of disease and every kind of sickness." (Matthew 9:35)

3) "And they healed all manner of sickness and all manner of diseases." (Matthew 10:1)

4) "But Jesus, aware of this, withdrew from there, and many followed Him, and He healed them all." (Matthew 12:15)

5) "And when He went ashore, He saw a great multitude, and felt compassion for them, and He healed their sick." (Matthew 14:14)

6) "And when the men of that place recognized Him, they sent into all that surrounding district and brought to Him all who were sick; and they began to entreat Him that they might just touch the fringe of His cloak; and as many as touched it were healed." (Matthew 14:36)

There is no record that one single person who came to Jesus was refused healing. Jesus healed them all! In such large crowds, you would think there might be one so wicked that He would refuse, but He didn't. Jesus made it clear to us that it is His will **for all** to receive healing. If Satan is lying to you and telling you that you can't receive healing because of what you've done, just picture yourself in the crowd, reaching out to Jesus. He would not have left you out then, and He won't now.

It can get discouraging if we think that Jesus was the only one who could heal the multitudes, because He was the Son of God. However, He is not the only one! Look at John 14:12: **"Truly I say to you, he who believes in Me, the works that I do shall he do also; and greater works than these shall he do; because I go the Father."** We believe in Jesus, so we are to pray for the sick and do the works of Jesus.

In Luke 10:1-9, we read that Jesus appointed seventy people and sent them to preach. In verse 9, He told them to **"Heal the sick that are there."** So, not only did the twelve disciples pray for the sick, but the seventy also. He later commissioned all believers to pray for the sick, as well as preach to them. **"And these** signs shall follow them that believe; in My name shall they lay hands on the sick, and they shall recover" (Mark 16:17-18). God was, and still is, very concerned for the sick. He made plenty of provision for people to be healed and to hear the whole gospel.

Let's look at five individual cases and how Jesus healed them:

1) **"And behold, there came a leper and worshiped him, saying, Lord, if you will, you can make me clean. And Jesus put forth his hand, and touched him saying, I will; be cleansed. And immediately the leprosy was cleansed."** (Matthew 8:2-3) Many people believe God is able, but they question if He really will. In this impossible situation of leprosy, Jesus states, **"I will it so,"** or **"It is My will."** As a parent I want my kids to be blessed—healthy physically and emotionally, and provided for. We are imperfect parents, but we want good for our children. God is the perfect parent who wants only good for us. I believe that just as I would not withhold good shoes from my kids if it were in my means to get them, God will not withhold what we need either. The scripture says, **"He will not withhold one good thing from those who trust in Him."** (Ps. 84:11) Again, there is not one example in the New Testament where Jesus refused to heal someone who came to Him. Jesus tells the leper, **"It is my will."** Jesus is speaking and demonstrating to us God's will to heal the sick.

2) **"Now when Jesus had come into Peter's house, He saw his wife's mother lying sick with a fever. So He touched her hand, and the fever left her. And she arose and served them."** (Matthew

8:14-15 NKJV) When you are sick, it is difficult to serve your family or anyone else. It can be hard to even pray or attend a church service. Sometimes I hear people say, "I learned such and such when I was sick." That may be true. God will use anything to bring you to Himself, but He desires you to be well. He can teach you things when you're well, too, if you'll listen to Him. When you're sick, it's hard to think about anyone else. Notice that "she arose and served them." When she was sick she couldn't minister to them, but healed she was a blessing. God wants us blessed in order to be a blessing.

3) **"And, behold, they brought to him a man sick of the palsy, lying on a bed; and Jesus seeing their faith said unto the sick of the palsy; Son, be of good cheer; your sins are forgiven. . . . Arise and walk. . . . "And he arose and departed to his house."** (Matthew 9:2-7) Jesus saw the friends' faith. We may have sick children or loved ones in a condition where they cannot seek God for themselves, but we can believe for and with them. My husband and I are particularly moved for parents with handicapped children. In many cases, the child cannot believe for himself, but the parents can. We prayed with the grandparents of a baby who was supposed to have Down's Syndrome. They stretched out their faith to God, really believing He would heal. The baby is completely normal today, and I believe it's because of the grandparents' faith and prayer!

Marty and I became friends with a couple who had a CMV (Cytomegalic Inclusion Virus) baby. The baby could not stretch to God in faith, but those parents could and did. They read the Word of God on healing to her daily. They talked to her like they would to a healthy baby. When we first saw them, their baby was three years old and she had no motor skills. She just lay on the pallet and did not move. They would put her in a baby walker and she slumped like a rag doll, but they refused to give up. They would say things to her like, "Grace, your legs are strong. Push yourself around. Your back is strong. Sit up, baby!" Guess what? She is four now, and she sits up, pushes herself around in the walker and rolls and scoots off the pallet! She is progressively receiving her healing. Remember, this is a disease the doctors call irreversible. She was blind and deaf until one year ago, but now she has 100% eyesight and hearing! Praise the Lord!

Sometimes healing takes time, because often it is progressive. John 4:46-53 tells us about a boy who "began to get better" or "began to mend." His healing was not instant, but took a little time.

4) **"Two blind men heard Jesus was passing by and cried out, saying, Have mercy on us, O Lord, thou Son of David! ...Jesus had compassion on them and touched their eyes; immediately their eyes received sight and they followed Him."** (Matthew 20:30-34) Jesus always had compassion on those who cried out after Him, and He still does today!

5) **Mark 5:22-43**—Jairus had a daughter at the point of death. He said to Jesus, "Come and lay hands on her, that she may be healed, and she will live." Even after the woman with the issue of blood interrupted their trip to his home, Jairus

stayed in faith. Even when his servant came and told him, "Your daughter is dead, don't bother Jesus anymore," he believed. This servant was a doubter, but Jesus said to Jairus, "Be not afraid; only believe." And Jairus received his daughter back. What a marvelous lesson for us to persevere in faith despite obstacles or setbacks. Jesus never turned anyone away.

Now let's look at a fuller understanding of our salvation:

A critical eye opener in my understanding of healing was when I discovered that the terms "save" and "salvation" do not only mean eternal salvation in heaven, but also healing—spirit, soul, and body. The word "salvation" is *soteria* in Greek, which *Vine's Expository Dictionary* defines as **deliverance, preservation, salvation, safety and health and soundness.**

Here are a few scriptures in this regard:

1) II Corinthians 6:2 "Now is the day of **salvation**."
   Or: "Now is the day of deliverance;" "Now is the day of health," and so on.
2) Acts 4:12 "Neither is there salvation in any other: for there is no other name under heaven given among men, whereby we must be **saved**."
3) Ephesians 1:13 "In Him you also trusted, after you heard the Word of truth, the gospel of your **salvation**; in whom also, having believed, you were sealed with the Holy Spirit of promise."
   Or: The good news of deliverance; the good news of healing.

From now on, when you see the word *salvation*, keep in mind that it includes **_DELIVERANCE, HEALTH, and SOUNDNESS!_**

The word "saved" in the Greek is *sozo*. **Sozo is translated, "will preserve." The very definition of**

"preserve" includes the whole person: spirit, soul, and body. I think that is something to shout about!

Oh, surely God didn't leave us on earth to just accept every nasty sickness, disease, and harmful thing that comes against us. He has always provided us healing and deliverance when we trust Him. That is the good news of the gospel. That is the abundant life Jesus talked about.

Here is the story of a lady who refused to live with disease in her body. One night up at the church, we had given a teaching on healing. Afterwards, this lady came up to receive prayer for healing. She had lupus. We prayed for her, and some days later, she came back with her lab reports showing that she no longer had lupus. She said she could run all over the place and chase her grandchildren. She keeps that report in her Bible to share her testimony of what God did for her.

There are many exciting verses to look at, interpret, and meditate on until we grasp their all-encompassing meanings, but let's just look at a few:

1) Matthew 9:22 In this story, the woman with the issue of blood receives her healing, and Jesus says, "Daughter, be of good comfort; your faith has **made you whole (or your faith has saved you)."**

2) Acts 14:9 In the story of the man lame from birth, the word in verse nine, "and perceiving that he had faith to be **healed**," is the **same Greek word sozo that is translated "saved" in Romans 10:9.**

3) Luke 7:36-50 This is the story of "a woman in the city, which was a sinner." She anoints Jesus at the Pharisee's house. In verse 48, Jesus says, "Your sins are forgiven." In verse 50, Jesus says, "Your faith has **saved you**; go in peace."

4) Luke 18:35-42 This passage is about a blind man who received his sight. Verse 42 says, "Receive your sight; your faith has **saved you**." Your faith has **saved you, healed you, and delivered you.**

The Word of God is very exciting when we really understand it. Do you know that Matthew 15:6 says, **"The traditions of men make the Word of God of no effect?"** How do our traditions make the Word of God powerless? When we believe wrongly, our unbelief actually can stop the power of God in our lives. Of course, God is so merciful that there are times when He completely overrides our wrong thinking or believing and moves out of His great compassion. But many times, the way we believe actually hinders God. For example, some people really believe a certain sin they've committed is the "unpardonable sin" and God cannot forgive them. They might think God cannot forgive adultery, so they believe that they have lost their salvation because of that moral failure. They could spend the rest of their lives very distant from God. That kind of thinking hinders God's work in their lives even though the Word of God says Jesus will forgive all our sins.

Incorrect thinking is one of the reasons many Christians live in defeat or have died prematurely, never receiving from God what they need. They were not accurately taught the Word of God. Yet look at the book of Acts. It is obvious to me that the believers in that day understood that Jesus came to save us, heal us, deliver us, and give us abundant life. This is not the Christianity many of us have heard about today. Many of us have only heard that we have eternal salvation, and that we have to spend this life just making it the best way we can until heaven. Jesus' followers in Acts understood more fully what He came to do—save, heal, and deliver "<u>on earth</u> as it is in heaven."

Look at the response of the people when they received the gospel from those early Christians. In Acts 3:1-9, a man who was lame from birth was instantly healed when Peter and John said, **"In the name of Jesus Christ of Nazareth rise up and walk."** Acts 5:12 states, **"Many signs and wonders were wrought by the apostles."** The power of God so operated through Peter that **"the people brought the sick into the streets...and they were healed, every one"** (Acts 5:15). Also, the people listened to Philip speak, **"hearing and seeing the miracles which he did"** (Acts 8:6-7). **"And God wrought special miracles by the hands of Paul"** (Acts 19:11).

The entire book of Acts is filled with the wonderful healing power of God operating through those who believe. The good news is that healing did not end with the Apostles. We can find accounts of healings in the writings of Tertullian, Origen, and Clement dated around the 3rd century A.D. There are many recorded miracles in the ministry of St. Francis of Assisi from the 1200s. One such story is about a leper colony where St. Francis and his monks fed, bathed and took care of the lepers. There was one leper who was so angry and bitter that when the monks would go in to change his dressing or to try to feed him, the man would curse and throw his food at them. They could not console him. Finally, St. Francis went in to the man and began telling him how much God loved him, how God wanted to touch him, and how Jesus had not forsaken him in his pain. As St. Francis spoke words of life over him and undressed his wounds, new flesh appeared. The angry man was completely healed and restored.

John Wesley, Maria Woodworth-Etter, Smith Wigglesworth, Aimee Semple McPherson, and many others in years gone by saw healings and miracles that we can now read about in books. Healing did not end with the Apostles. God has continued healing through the centuries, and He does the same for us today. As we believe God, He works miracles for us, too!

CHAPTER 5

Misconceptions about Healing

Now we understand that the Word is true. It provides healing for us. Jesus came to manifest the will of God on earth, and He healed "them all"—*all* includes *you*. Let's look at some common misconceptions that keep you from having faith in Jesus and His Word for healing. I believe it is important to be honest with yourself and God and say, "I am stuck here," or, "I'm not sure about this." Study and pray about it. Don't let it continue to cloud your believing. The following pages address some common misconceptions that hinder people in believing God. They arise mostly from traditional teachings or wrong conclusions not based on scripture but on human reasoning.

Misconception #1
Paul's "thorn in the flesh" was a sickness that God would not take away.

Many people say that Paul's thorn in the flesh was a sickness that God did not heal. My religion professor in college told our class that it was believed that Paul had an eye disease. I had a hard time with this, because when Paul got born again, Ananias laid hands on his blind eyes, and he was healed. I couldn't imagine Paul being healed only partially by the Lord through Ananias. There are also no scriptures telling us that Paul had an eye disease or any other sickness. We know that Paul was greatly used of God to heal the sick during his lifetime. Acts 28:8 says, "Paul, who was on the island of Miletus, prayed for all the sick, and they were healed."

My belief is that God permitted this "thorn in the flesh" to come upon Paul, but it was not from Him. The bible specifically says that it was "a messenger of Satan." And James 1:12 says, "Let no man say when he is tempted, I am tempted of God; for God cannot be tempted with evil, <u>neither does He tempt any man!</u>"

In II Corinthians 12:7, we learn that "a <u>messenger</u> of Satan was permitted to buffet" him. The word *messenger* here is the Greek word *angels,* meaning a personality or an angel of Satan, not a disease! *Buffet* means *to hit or give repeated blows.* The "messenger of Satan" was sent to stop the Word of God from being preached by repeated blows. Everywhere Paul went, the "messenger" stirred up persecution, jail sentences, shipwrecks, and many other attacks. There is a thorough list in II Corinthians 11:23-29 of the persecutions Paul went through. Sickness is not listed. "Buffeted" is also used in Matthew 26:67 and Mark 14:65 to refer to repeated blows, not sickness. Weymouth's translation of II Corinthians 12:7 reads, "There was given me a thorn in the flesh, Satan's angel to deal blows at me."

Paul sought the Lord three times that he might get it to depart from him. God responded to him in verse 9, "My grace is sufficient for you, for power is perfected in weaknesses."

The Amplified says in verse 9, "But He said to me, My grace—My favor and loving-kindness and mercy are enough for you, [that is, sufficient against any danger and to enable you to bear the trouble manfully]; for My strength and power are made perfect—fulfilled and completed and show themselves most effective—in your weakness."

Paul suffered a lot of trouble in his life, but disease was never on the list. Let's go ahead and look at II Corinthians 11...

24 Five times I received from the Jews 39 lashes.
25 Three times I was beaten with rods, once I was stoned; three times I was shipwrecked, a night and a day I have spent in the deep.
26 I have been on frequent journeys, in dangers from rivers, danger from robbers, danger from my countrymen, dangers from the Gentiles, dangers in the city, danger in the wilderness, dangers on the sea, dangers among false brethren;
27 I have been in labor and hardship, through many sleepless nights, in hunger and thirst, often without food, in cold and exposure..."

Jesus did not promise to take away the buffetings or persecution, but even in persecutions, God wants us to remember: **"Many are the afflictions of the righteous but I will deliver them out of them all"** (Psalm 34:19).

Paul said in II Timothy 3:11-12, "...Persecutions and sufferings, such as happened to me at Antioch and Iconium and at Lystra; what persecutions I endured, and out of them all the Lord delivered me!" And indeed, all who desire to live godly in Christ Jesus will be persecuted." We hear so much more about the thorn in the flesh than the outcome of those trials. Here Paul declares, **"The Lord delivered me <u>out of them all</u>."** He won! It didn't say he never went without food, because he did. But he was delivered. He lived to be an old man. There are differing views on Paul's thorn in the flesh, but I believe a main point here is that Paul walked in a lot of victory even in the most difficult of situations, and he kept preaching and healing everywhere he went.

Whatever you believe about Paul's thorn in the flesh, the comforting passage, **"My grace is sufficient for you,"** applies to us all. Whatever sickness, attack, or difficulty may come, God is enough! His mercy prevails; His grace and provision will get us through.

Misconception #2
God puts sickness on people to teach them something.

This is a very common misconception of God's character. If God put a disease on a person, and they believe it is not God's will to heal them, then why do they go to the doctor for healing? Why do they use medicine? Wouldn't it be fighting against God's will for that person to go to the doctor or hospital for help? That is crazy! Medicine and doctors are a good gift *from God*, and He often uses them in our healing. Unfortunately, some people have refused treatment because they failed to realize that medicine is from God. People have died of simple illnesses that medicine could have cured because they thought it more spiritual to suffer.

Now, if there were a person who purposely put cancer or AIDS on another human being, that person would be put in prison. Yet, we say God does. I've heard people say that God caused so and so to have a car wreck and break his arm and leg to get his attention. This is inconsistent with God's Word and His character. If I caused my husband to have a wreck to get his attention, I would be in serious legal trouble, not to mention relationship trouble.

No! God's Word declares in Jeremiah 29:11 and in many other places, **"For I know the plans that I have for you, plans for welfare and not for calamity to give you a future and a hope."** It isn't God's plan to make life difficult and filled with suffering and heartache. Jesus said He came **"to give life and life more abundantly."**

The word *life* in the Greek means *the God kind of life*. God will use everything in our lives to speak to us, help us and reveal Himself to us, but I don't believe it is consistent with His character to cause bad and hurtful things.

There is a huge difference between God permitting something and God commissioning something. For example, God might permit someone to drink, use drugs, or steal, etc., but He definitely doesn't commission it. I hear a lot of people saying, "Well, you know God allowed so and so to get cancer." The truth is that God will allow you to go to hell if you want, but He doesn't want you to.

This misconception is very immobilizing to the church because it causes people to drop their weapons and leave the fight. Ephesians 6 tells us to put on the armor of God and stand against the onslaught of the enemy. If we take everything life throws at us and think it is God doing it, we will take a lot of hits from the enemy that we do not need to.

God is not going to use the devil to care for or teach His children. **"The devil is out to kill, steal, and destroy"** (John 10:10), and sickness can be one of his ways to destroy people.

What does the bible say God uses to teach His people? Ephesians 4:11 says, **"And He gave some, apostles and some, prophets; and some, evangelists; and some, pastors, and teachers; for the <u>perfecting</u> of the saints, for the work of the ministry, for the edifying of the body of Christ."** *Perfecting* means a process leading to completeness, or fulfillment. The five-fold ministry operating through people God puts in our lives teaches us, not sickness and disease.

Misconception #3
People are "suffering for Jesus" in their sickness.

Another way of putting it is that they are glorifying God in their sickness. Sickness <u>does not</u> glorify God. The parents of a friend of mine loved God, but they were never taught to stand on the Word, especially not for healing. Their pastor and his wife suffered many diseases as well, and thought these sicknesses were God's will. The pastor's wife finally died from diabetes, and when she died, her legs had so decayed that church members wrapped them in plastic to contain the smell. She had refused to go to the doctor because she was "suffering for Jesus".

My friend was young at the time, but still remembers wondering what was gained by her pastor's wife "suffering for Jesus." She couldn't understand the reasoning behind having a leg infected with gangrene, with its pain and stench—all for Jesus.

"And great multitudes came to Him, bringing with them those who were lame, crippled, blind, dumb, and many others, and they laid them down at His feet; and He healed them, so that the multitude marveled as they saw the dumb speaking, the crippled restored, and the lame walking, and the blind seeing; and they glorified the God of Israel" (Matthew 15:30-32).

What glorifies God? John 15:8 says, **"Herein is my Father glorified, that you bear much fruit."** Never does the Bible indicate anywhere that sickness glorifies Him. If sickness glorifies God, then why would Jesus deny God so much glory by healing everyone who came to Him? Did those decaying legs glorify God? I believe God has given us doctors and excellent medicines.

One marvelous healing story I heard that made me shout and glorify God was of a boy who was healed of a severe neurological disease. He was born completely healthy, played sports, and did well at school, but around the age of 7, he began having seizures and his health quickly deteriorated. He reached the point that he was unable to do schoolwork or even attend school because of constant jerking motions and the inability to control his emotions. From the beginning of his illness, he was cognizant of God and sought prayer for his healing. Before his 15th birthday, he announced to his family that he believed he would be healed on his birthday. His parents did not want to discourage him, so they refrained from saying anything negative, but were very concerned about his feelings if no change occurred. The night of his birthday, his mother was awakened by a very strong, tangible presence of God in the house; something they had never experienced before. She did not get up because she knew it was her son's moment. Sure enough, the next morning, he came to breakfast completely healed! He finished his education in a public high school in regular classes and even resumed playing sports. You would never know he suffered from this disease.

Misconception #4
It may not be God's will to heal.

The Bible is God's Word, His will and testament. God's Word on a matter is His will and His desire for you. We have already studied many verses in the Old and New Testaments that prove to us God's will for us to be healed. When the Israelites came out of Egypt, the

Bible says, **"There was not one feeble person among them"** (Psalm 105:37). Jesus healed the multitudes and so did Paul. In all those millions of Israelites and in the multitudes in Jesus' day, there were none that God did not want to heal. And possibly now, *you're* the exception? I don't think so! <u>I know</u> Jesus wants you well!

God has already given us His Word for healing, so we do not need to pray, *"If it be Your will...."* That is like asking, "Is it Your will to keep Your Word?" We ask God to show us His will about things on which His Word is not clear, such as, "Do I marry John?" "Do I go to college in this town?" "Do I major in education?" But with so many scriptures on healing, we can know without a doubt that God is very concerned with our lives and wanting to heal us. Psalms 107:20 says, **"He sent His Word and healed them, and delivered them from all their destructions."**

Say out loud: Thank You, Jesus; it is Your will that I walk in perfect health. Thank You for healing my body, now. Thank You for sending Your Word and healing me. In Jesus Name, Amen.

Misconception #5
People receive sickness because of past sins.

Isaiah 43:25	**"I, yes, I alone, am the One who blots out your sins for My own sake and will never think of them again."** The NIV states, **"I will remember your sins no more."**
Psalm 103:12	**"As far as the east is from the west, so far has He removed our transgressions from us."**

II Corinthians
5:17-19   **"Therefore if any man be in Christ, he is a new creature: old things are passed away, behold, all things are become new. And all things are of God, <u>who has reconciled us to Himself by Jesus Christ</u>, and has given to us the ministry of reconciliation. For God was in Christ, reconciling the world to Himself, no longer counting people's sins against them."**

So God is saying to us that if anyone accepts Jesus as Lord, as the One sent in payment for his sin, he gets a fresh start; he is created new. The old life is gone; a new life begins. God settled the relationship between Himself and us forever.

I remember when Anna Joy was sick, my husband asked what we did to allow or cause this to happen. My father-in-law wisely told us the right question instead is, "What do we do now?" I also struggled at times early on with thoughts like, "Maybe I drank too many soft drinks or did something wrong that caused it." I had to get some peace by asking God to forgive me and leave the lingering negative thoughts with Him. Then I would ask God to fight for her. Sometimes looking back can cause you to feel so badly about yourself and your mistakes that you can't believe God would help you. Philippians 3:13 says we should be **"forgetting what is behind and straining toward the goal to win the prize for which God has called me heavenward in Christ Jesus."**

I have some friends with a wonderful story of God's forgiveness and deliverance along these lines. This couple grew up in a church where both their dads were deacons. They had learned right from wrong, but still made a mistake, and at age fifteen found out they were pregnant. Jerry (not his real name) said that one of the worst days of his life was when he had to tell his godly father that he had failed him, his girlfriend, and God in this way. The girl's parents supported her, and she finished high school while living at home and taking care of her baby with their help. The boy's parents did not want them to see each other, so he did not see the baby until she was eighteen months old. They began to date again their senior year of high school and got married at nineteen. They had wanted to marry, not only because of their daughter, but because they really loved each other. Shortly after they married, however, Jerry tried his first drug: methamphetamine. He became addicted for 4½ years. The progression of sin continued until it destroyed their lives with anger, abuse and more immorality. Finally, very broken and feeling hopeless, they cried out to Jesus to deliver them and save their family. Jerry confessed his sins and his great need for Jesus to deliver him from his addictions, anger, and selfishness. God instantly delivered him from the drug addiction! They began to pour themselves into God's Word daily, and to attend church, and develop deep accountability relationships there. It's now been several years, and he has never gone back. He and his wife have a very sweet relationship, and their family is completely restored with not even a residue of the past. Their daughter is a beautiful teenager now, very secure, godly, and full of life. She is Anna Joy's good friend.

Jerry does not call himself an addict or a recovering addict. He feels strongly that he is a new creation in Christ Jesus and the old things have passed away. He is forgetting the past and pressing on toward everything

God has for him. Because of this, he and his family are a blessing to many. I love it when he gives his testimony and helps us on Healing Night at church by praying with hurting people. His family's story is one of many wonderful miracles God is doing. God is a delivering God!! My friend often reminds me to please pray for the broken hearts as much as for the physically sick because he knows too well the pain and heartache that only Jesus can heal and restore.

"He bore our sicknesses" (Isaiah 53:4). If we do not choose to accept that Jesus bearing our sins and diseases was enough, how could we think that our carrying (or bearing) sickness or sin would be enough to please God? That is like saying, "God, I see Jesus carried my sins, but I've been so bad that I'd better carry them, too." **NO! Jesus is enough!** Put these false traditions behind you. Do not believe these lies any longer. They are a false belief system propagated by the devil to keep God's people sick. Believe the Bible and not these old lies that are designed to steal and stop your faith.

Confess out loud: *Lord, thank You for forgiving me of all my sins. Your Word says that if I ask You to forgive me, You are faithful and just to forgive me! Your Word says You put my sin in the sea of forgetfulness and You will not remember them again. Because of Jesus taking my place, I can come to You and expect You to answer my prayer. Lord, heal my body and my mind. Make me strong and free from all sickness and sin. Thank You. In Jesus Name, Amen.*

CHAPTER 6

Growing in Faith

The first step to growing in faith for healing is to know what the Bible teaches—that God is a healing God who delights in healing people.

Faith is expecting God's goodness and compassion to move on our behalf. Jesus was moved with compassion for the sick. Sometimes it is hard to believe for healing if our hearts condemn us for known sin. But we don't have to get discouraged. James 5:16 says, **"Confess your faults one to another, <u>that you may be healed."</u>** Proverbs 3:7-8 says, **"Fear the Lord, and depart from evil. It will be health to your body and marrow to your bones."**

It is very interesting to note in Luke 5:17-24 that Jesus first says, **"Your sins are forgiven."** Then, Jesus says, **"Arise, and take up your bed...."** In John 5:8, Jesus declares the same thing to a different man He has already healed; He tells him not to continue in sin.

That is good news for us. We can be forgiven and healed at the same time. Jesus healed the multitudes, so do not get under condemnation and get stuck looking at all your shortcomings. He does not expect you to be perfect to be healed.

Surely, the multitudes in Jesus' day and in Paul's day were dealing with sin issues, too, but mercifully God forgave them and healed them. Romans 5:8 says, **"While we were yet sinners, Christ died for us."** When your heart convicts you of sin, repent and ask God to forgive you. If you feel in your heart that you need to ask someone to forgive you—do it! Remember that Jesus took our place on the cross for forgiveness of sin. We accept that His payment places us in right standing before God.

Understanding Faith

We use faith everyday. We sit in a chair at the breakfast table without checking to see if it will hold us up. We put our kids on the bus for school believing it will take them to school. Faith believes something we do not see. Somehow we often think of faith or "great faith" as a hocus-pocus power, something not really attainable. We believe that faith is good, but too hard to get. God never intended faith to be so complicated or unattainable for us, because He tells us in Hebrews 11:6, **"Without faith, it is impossible to please God."**

At this time you may not have very much confidence in your own faith. In other words, you do not consider yourself to be a person of strong faith. Maybe you think strong faith is for those special called ones or for the very religious and pious, but not for the average schoolteacher, dad, or child. The good news is that all of us have been given faith by God. Romans 12:3 says, **"...God has dealt to every man the measure of faith."** So, if you are born again, you have faith!

The Bible tells us how our faith can grow. Romans 10:17 says, **"So then faith comes by hearing, and hearing by the Word of God."** It also says in 2 Thessalonians 1:3 **"that our faith can grow exceedingly."**

To recap:

1) Each of us has been given faith by God
2) Our faith can grow
3) Our faith grows by hearing, and hearing by the Word of God.

Let's look at the Bible's definition of faith. Hebrews 11:1 says, **"Now faith is the substance of things hoped for, the evidence of things not seen."**

1) **Now** - at the present time; immediately.
2) **Faith** - firm persuasion; a conviction based upon hearing; persuasion or conviction of the truthfulness of God; expectation or confidence; assurance; belief; faithfulness.
3) **Substance** - one's goods or possessions; property or writ of ownership.
4) **Hope** - confident expectation; having to do with the unseen and the future; the happy anticipation of good.
5) **Evidence** - proof; conviction.

Hebrews 11:1 (Moffatt's) says, **"Now faith means that we are <u>confident</u> of what we hope for, convinced of what we do not see." Confident** - a standing under; the quality of confidence which leads one to stand under, endure, or undertake anything; signifying substance.

Hebrews 11:1 (Amplified) says, **"Now faith is the assurance (the confirmation; the title deed) of the things we hope for, being the proof of things we do not see and the conviction of their reality—<u>faith perceiving as real fact what is not revealed to the senses."</u>**

When some people get a sickness or disease, they cry and plead with God to do something to heal them. They may recite all the good things they or the one for whom they are praying has done. Or they may do the opposite, saying,"Oh God, You know I'm nothing, but if You heal me, I'll serve You." People bargain with God when they are desperate.

This is not faith. Faith is saying in your heart, "Jesus, it is only because of You and Your payment on the cross that I can come to You. There is nothing of myself—what I have done or what I can do in the future, that can earn it. You came to earth, suffered for me, and took the stripes on Your back for me to receive healing. You paid for what I could not earn or pay for. I receive by faith my healing. Thank You for paying for it for me."

Picture in your mind Jesus on the cross taking all the sins of the world and all the diseases that would come. He took them on the cross. He paid for the sins and sicknesses of this world. We have to receive it by faith based on the Word of God and not our understanding. I love what it says in 1 Corinthians 2:8: "If they would have known, they would not have crucified the Lord of Glory." What Jesus paid for was amazing. Now, the only weapon the devil has is to deceive us, to stop us from seeing past the natural to see by faith. We must see what we are praying for in the spirit first, then in the natural. We have to change our thinking because God is a supernatural God, not a natural God.

How do we pray? In *faith*, not *need!* The Bible says in Mark 11:24, **"Therefore, I say unto you, what things so ever you desire, when you pray, believe that you receive them, and you shall have them."**

Let's look very carefully at this verse:
"What things so ever you desire,"
I desire to be healed.
"When you pray,"
I pray to be made whole.
"Believe that you receive."
I believe I receive my healing. I believe my body is healthy. I believe every cell in my body is healthy. There is no disease in my body. I will live long on the earth and declare His glory.

This is so contrary to our natural mind. Here are some principles to implement while you believe for healing:

#1 desire
#2 pray

#3 believe you receive
#4 see it manifested

Most people want it manifested first before they will believe. That is not biblical faith. Look for these principles when you read your Bible. Read the book of Joshua and notice how many times God tells Joshua "I have given you this land" before he ever had it. How many times did Joshua tell the people "God has given us this land" before they ever had it?

"Faith is the substance of things hoped for, the evidence of things not seen" (Hebrews 11:1). It is challenging in this life to walk in the Spirit because so much of our life is natural. We need to work, pay bills, be disciplined to study our Bibles, pray, and be unselfish. We need to take care of our relationships and spend time with loved ones, plus take care of our cars and houses. There's a balance of taking care of these things while still cultivating a life in the Spirit to have our ear towards heaven and hear God. The apostle Paul actually rebukes the Christians at Corinth for living "like mere men." Paul made tents to support himself financially, but gave everything else he had to preach the Word and walk with God. He is a great example to us of a responsible spiritual man. God is calling us to a deeper place in Him.

I have a friend who is a nurse practitioner, and she is very professional. She takes care of a lot of patients each day, but always has her ear towards heaven. Many times she will be taking care of a patient, and the Spirit of God will show her something she did not know about the person, such as the patient being in an abusive relationship or having an addiction. Once she was treating a patient based on the symptoms, but just as she was about to release her, she felt God tell her the problem even though the symptoms did not match up with it. She sent the woman to a specialist right away, and the specialist sent a message back that she had saved the woman's life. I believe God wants to walk intimately with us in our every day life—at our jobs, with our children—hearing Him day in and day out. We have to cultivate a life tuned to the Spirit even in the middle of doing the natural things of life.

Faith is perceiving as real fact what is not revealed to the senses. Faith looks "not at the things seen." If you have a severely handicapped child, the Bible tells us not to look at the disabilities. Look at God's ability!

I Corinthians 1:28 "... God has chosen ... the things which are not, so that He may nullify [bring to nothing, zero] the things that are..."

II Corinthians 4:18 "While we look not at the things which are seen, but at the things which are not seen; for the things that are seen are temporal [subject to change]; but the things which are not seen are eternal."

According to 1 Peter 2:24, **"By His stripes I am healed."** My senses may not know it, but I possess it in the Spirit, because the Word is truer than what I see. God's Word alone is our reason for believing that our prayer is answered before we see or feel it. This is faith!

Good testimonies encouraged my faith tremendously. Dodie Osteen, a pastor's wife from Lakewood Church in Houston, recorded a testimony of her healing from cancer. She was diagnosed with metatastic cancer of the liver, meaning that it had spread throughout her body. She was sent home to die within a few weeks, but she stood on God's promises and was healed. When we were going through Anna Joy's illness, I listened to that tape almost daily. I also listened to tapes from my favorite teachers who taught the Word and faith. I constantly had good teaching going in even when I was doing laundry or cooking dinner. It became a lifestyle for us. When I listened my faith grew strong, and I was ready to fight and win.

I would think, "Well, if God can do it for Dodie Osteen, he can do it for us." My faith always gets pumped up when I listen to good Word teaching.

A few years ago a huge tornado went through Lancaster, Texas where my sister lived. She was standing with my dad outside her house, and she yelled out loud, "I plead the blood of Jesus over my house and I command that tornado not to touch my house, in Jesus' Name!" The very minute she finished praying, the tornado started down the street toward them. The sound was almost deafening. She and my dad ran into the house to the bathroom and were extremely frightened as the tornado blew by. She thought, "What happened to my faith? So much for being a faith woman." But you know what? That tornado went right over her house. It didn't touch her home, but it uprooted the big beautiful trees along the creek behind her house, severely damaged houses in her neighborhood, and flattened most of downtown Lancaster, too.

My sister prayed a faith-filled prayer. It was powerful and effective as James 5:16 says. We still have emotions and fear at times, but as we keep our eyes on Jesus—on His strength and power—we will know that He is more than enough to get us over even if we break down at times.

Asking in Faith

When you go to God to heal your body or mind, whatever the need is, you need to be convinced that it is God's will by the Word of God. Now, don't make that harder than it is. If God said it, it's settled. Don't ask Him if it's His will again. Go in faith. Say out loud, *"God, Your Word says not to forget my benefits of forgiveness and health based on Psalm 103:2-3. Therefore, I come to You as Your child and receive by faith the healing I need. Thank You for hearing me, Lord. Amen."*
Meditate on the following scriptures:

1) Matthew 7:11 "If you then, being evil, know how to give good gifts to your children, how much more shall your Father which is in heaven give good things to them that ask Him?" **Expect good.**
2) Matthew 21:21-22 "And Jesus answered and said to them, "Truly I say to you, if you have faith and do not doubt, you will not only do what was done to the fig tree, but even if you say to this mountain, 'Be taken up and cast into the sea,' it will happen. And all things you ask in prayer, believing, you will receive." **Doubt not.**
3) Luke 11:9-10 "And I say unto you, ask, and it shall be given you; seek, and you shall find; knock, and it shall be opened unto you. For everyone that asks receives; and he that seeks finds; and to him that knocks it shall be opened." **Ask in faith.**
4) John 14:13-14 "And whatsoever you shall ask in My name, that will I do, that the Father may be glorified in the Son. If you shall ask anything in My name, I will do it." **He will do it.**

5) John 15:7 "If you abide in Me, and My words abide in you, you shall ask what you will, and it shall be done unto you." ***It shall be done.***

6) John 16:23 "Whatsoever you shall ask in My name, He [the Father] will give it you." ***He will give it.***

7) I John 3:22 "And whatsoever we ask, we receive of Him, because we keep His commandments, and do those things that are pleasing in His sight." ***We receive of Him.***

8) I John 5:14-15 "And this is the confidence that we have in Him, that if we ask anything according to His will, He hears us; and if we know that He hears us, whatsoever we ask, we know that we have the petitions that we desired of Him." ***We have the petitions.***

My husband Marty had eczema as a child. It was so bad that he had to take medicated baths, and his parents wrapped his ankles and wrists in plastic to keep him from scratching in his sleep. He still has large scars on his ankles from scratching as a child until he bled. For the first eight years we were married his hands were always cracked, red, and swollen looking. Marty got tired of it and really got serious about asking God to heal him. He wrote out healing scriptures and prayed them out loud several times a day. He would pray, "Thank you, God, for healing my hands, for causing them not to crack, for causing them to be healthy." For the last ten years, his hands have been normal. God healed them. Our fourth daughter Lindsey had eczema. Even when she was just crawling she scratched her ankles and wrists until they bled. God had taught us not only to pray for healing but also to speak His Word out loud, thanking Him for her healing even before we saw it.

Praise God, her skin was healed as a small child so that she doesn't have to suffer years with a skin disorder like the diagnosis predicted. We are so thankful God heals!

You might ask, "What do I do if the symptoms don't leave or change?" Jesus asked, **"When I come back to the earth will I find faith?"** (Luke 18:8) I'd rather believe God for something than to be lazy and not stretch in believing for the supernatural. We still deal with asthma with Lindsey, yet when we give her the medicine we pray, "God, we know You are a supernatural God! We know You love us and care for every detail. Jesus, You paid an expensive price for us! Thank You that by Your stripes, Lindsey is healed. Thank You for healing her lungs and causing her to breathe well! Thank You that her body responds healthily to outside substances. She is well, healed, and whole in every way!"

We still give her the medicine if she needs it, but we continue to keep the switch of faith turned on. Everyday we expect the asthma to leave her, and when it doesn't yet, we keep right on praying and declaring God's Word. Healing is a good benefit (Ps 103:2-3), but it is not all there is to God. In the waiting, we love Him, we're growing, and we're seeking Him and His ways for our lives.

Let's look at some biblical examples of faith. Hebrews 11 tells us about many of them, and is often referred to as the faith chapter. Hebrews 11:7 says, **"By faith Noah, being warned of God of things not seen as yet..."** Noah believed God's Word and prepared the ark without ever seeing rain. Some Bible scholars say that he did not even know what rain was. Verse 8 says, **"By faith, Abraham...obeyed; and he went out, not knowing where to go."** Moses, moved by faith, went to Pharaoh to free the Hebrew slaves. Verse 29 says,

"By faith they passed through the Red Sea." And verse 30 says of Joshua and the Hebrews, **"By faith the walls of Jericho fell down."**

Those miracles were not the result of a "sit-in-your-chair" kind of belief. They were from faith in action! Belief moved into action and became faith. None of these heroes of faith had only a mental belief. They acted out their faith and the miracles came. That kind of faith performs miracles. Faith without corresponding action is dead. Real faith speaks *and* acts!

Let's look at more examples and ask ourselves, "What does faith look like?"

"And when Jesus entered Capernaum, a centurion came to Him, imploring Him, and saying, "Lord, my servant is lying paralyzed at home, fearfully tormented." Jesus said to him, "I will come and heal him." But the centurion said, " Lord, I am not worthy for You to come under my roof, but just say the word, and my servant will be healed. For I also am a man under authority, with soldiers under me; and I say to this one, 'Go!' and he goes, and to another, 'Come!' and he comes, and to my slave, 'Do this!' and he does it." Now when Jesus heard this, He marveled and said to those who were following, "Truly I say to you, I have not found such great faith with anyone in Israel"

(Matthew 8:5-10).

Why did Jesus say that the centurion had great faith? Look at verse 8. Here the centurion says, **"Speak the word only, and my servant will be healed."** This man understood the authority Jesus had from God. His word had authority. The same is true today. We need to have great faith in God and His Word today.

Mark 2:5 describes a man sick with palsy. The man's friends tried to take him to Jesus, but the place was too crowded. They tore the roof apart and let the man down right in front of Jesus. Verse 5 says, **"When Jesus saw their faith."** He could see their faith by their actions.

Look at the faith of Jairus, a ruler of the synagogue. He came to Jesus **"and begged Him earnestly, saying, "My little daughter lies at the point of death. Come and lay Your hands on her, that she may be healed, and she will live"** (Mark 5:22, NKJV).

That was faith talking. He knew that if Jesus came his daughter would be fine. Jesus went with him, and on the way a woman who had had an issue of blood for twelve years "had heard of Jesus, pressed in behind and touched his garment. **"For she kept saying, if I touch his garment, I shall be whole"** (Mark 5:27-28). And she was healed! Jesus stopped to see who received the healing from Him. Mark 5:34 says, **"Daughter, your faith has made you whole."**

According to Hebrew custom, this woman could have been stoned for going out in public with an issue of blood. So she was acting in faith to begin with when she went outside to pursue Jesus even though she knew it would be unacceptable. She was also continually talking to herself in faith—"If I touch him, I'll be healed." And in her anemic condition, she had to press through the throng of people around Jesus to get to Him. She would not stop until she got her miracle. And she did!

Consider Jairus during that delay. We can tell he was desperate for Jesus to hurry, because he said, "She lies at the point of death" (Mark 5:23). Then someone from his house came and said, "Your daughter is dead, why trouble the master any further?" (Mark 5:35). He could have given up! Jesus said to him, **"Be not afraid; only believe"** (Mark 5:36). Believing even after his daughter was dead must have been very hard. But he kept going with Jesus. Even when the people laughed at him, he didn't give up, and he got his miracle.

Both Jairus and the woman with the issue of blood had faith that was active. Despite obstacles, they kept pressing into Jesus and expecting to receive from Him. We need to be that way.

Let's look at faith in one more example. In Matthew 15:22-28, there is a woman who cried out to Jesus to heal her daughter who was "grievously vexed with a devil." At first, Jesus did not respond to her, so she continued to cry out after Him. Finally, He told her, "I was sent only to the lost sheep of the house of Israel" (verse 24). Jesus really put her off, so *she could have given up*. But instead, she **"came and worshiped Him, saying, Lord, help me"** (verse 25). He continued to tell her, "It is not proper to take the children's bread, and to cast it to dogs" (verse 26). He basically called her a dog. How many would have had their feelings hurt and left? Not this woman! She was desperate! She said, "Truth Lord: yet even the dogs eat of the crumbs which fall from their master's table" (verse 27). Then Jesus answered, **"O woman, great is your faith; be it done for you as you wish.' And her daughter was made well from that very hour"** (Verse 28).

Perseverance

We need to be a persevering people—to keep seeking, pressing, believing; speaking the Word until the answer comes. Do not give up. Nothing is impossible with God. These kinds of miracles happen today. I know of a pastor who was diagnosed with prostate cancer. After he got all the test results back, he shut himself in his house listening to healing tapes, meditating on the Word, and confessing the Word out loud over his body. He was diligent about digging into healing. After one week he went back in and told the doctor to do the tests again. The results showed no sign of cancer. Hallelujah!

Jesus said that **"we ought always to pray and not to turn coward (faint, lose heart, and give up)"** (Luke 18:1 AMP). We give up too easily. We need to mature so that we can endure through the difficult times. That's why we need to read and study our Bible. Our faith grows as we read and hear the Word of God. I encourage you to read through the first four books of the New Testament to see the actions of faith by those who were healed. Most of these people actively went to Jesus with faith to be healed. They were not just sitting by and hoping that perhaps He would heal them. They went after it! You go after it, saying it out loud: *Yes, God, I believe You will do for me just like You have done for them.*

Real Faith is Action

In James 2:17 we read, **"Even so faith without corresponding action is dead."** Moffatt's translation says, **"I will show you by my actions what faith is."**

I saw great example of faith in action during a time in a Sunday service when we prayed for the sick. A young college student came up to me for prayer. She had dyslexia, and had struggled terribly, attending twelve different schools, and even a boarding school to try to graduate from high school. In college, she was in a special program, but it was very difficult for her. We prayed, and I did not feel a thing. She said she felt "two things connect in my brain." A friend of mine asked her to try to read. She did right then, and could read perfectly for the first time. The next week she made her first "A" on a college exam. I still see her occasionally, and we rejoice together over what God did.

I Thessalonians 2:13 says, **"The Word of God which effectually works in you that believe."** When His Word convinces us that our prayer is answered, even before we have seen the answer, God's Word is stirring and changing us. It is "effectually working in us" to manifest health.

CHAPTER 7

Speaking the Word

The principle of speaking God's Word is greatly misunderstood. This is unfortunate, since it is a powerful truth that works victory in our lives. As we have studied in previous chapters, faith without corresponding action is useless. Faith is released in our words and actions. Jesus defeated the devil in the wilderness by speaking God's Word out loud. He said "It is written," and we must do the same. I believe that if faith is only in our head and not acted upon or spoken, it will not usually change circumstances.

Let's look at a few key scriptures in regard to the spoken word:

Proverbs 18:21	**"The tongue has the power of life and death and those who love it will eat its fruit."**
Matthew 12:36-37	**"For by your words you shall be justified, and by your words you shall be condemned."**
Mark 11:22	**"Have faith in God. For assuredly, I say to you, whoever says to this mountain, 'Be removed and be cast into the sea,' and does not doubt in his heart, but believes that those things he says will be done, he will have whatever he says."** (NKJV)

Mark 11:22 scripture mentions the word "says" four times. This is very powerful. The mountains can be the

trials in our lives. Sometimes we need to speak to them and not just pray. In my experience, after I've prayed about something for quite a while, I will feel a secure place with God, and my prayer then changes to more of a declaration.

Here is an example of how I pray for my girls. I have four incredibly godly girls. If I am concerned about peer pressure on their hearts, I pray, "Lord, I lift up my girls to You today. I pray that they would hear Your voice. I pray they would be sensitive to Your spirit to cling to what is good and flee from evil. I pray they have kind, godly friends to walk with at school and enjoy the life You have for them." Then I would transition after awhile and declare the Word. I would pray something like this: "I thank You, God, that my girls love You with all their hearts, minds, souls, and strength. They are bold witnesses for You, declaring holiness and righteousness. They are bold against peer pressure - standing up for righteousness. They are marked by Your presence, Your glory, and Your favor. They are mighty young women of God!" These are not empty words spoken with presumption; they are God's heart. They come not out of my head, but out of my relationship with Jesus - out of my spirit.

Faith is not the same as hope. Hebrews 11:1 says, "Now faith." If faith is not present tense, but rather out there in the future, it is not faith, but hope. Hope means *earnest expectation*. Hope is critically important to our journey of faith. You have to have hope for the thing you need and to expect earnestly for it. But if you stay in hope and do not reach faith, you could spend your lifetime hoping it away. When I think of, "earnest expectation," I think of a child reaching his neck out the door, stretching to see if his dad or grandma is there yet. It is an expectation.

One writer says about Hebrews 11:1, **"Faith is laying hold of the unrealities of hope and bringing them into the realm of reality." Faith says the same thing the Word of God says!**

Hope is always future tense. Faith is now—present tense! If you say that you believe, but you are seeing it in the future instead of in the present, then you're not believing; you are hoping. Faith believes that He has done it and is doing it! "Jesus died on the cross for the forgiveness of sins, that we, being dead to sins, should live unto righteousness; **by whose stripes you were healed!"** (I Peter 2:24)

Yes, it is done (past tense)! *I'm healed. I'm forgiven. I'm more than a conqueror because Jesus paid the price.* Now I'm not talking about saying it to everyone around you. I'm talking primarily about your own prayer time, when you are in your house throwing in the laundry, or driving in your car. You don't have to say things around people. It is between you and God. Declare it in the heavenlies in your private time.

I've heard this little formula for faith patterned after Abraham's faith: "First, he had God's Word for it. Second, he believed God's Word. Third, he considered not the contradictory circumstances. Fourth, he gave praise to God."

Real faith is based on the Word of God. If God says it, it is settled forever! When we were in the heat of the battle over Anna Joy, my husband and I turned off the television. We didn't read the newspaper. We studied our Bible on healing, read good books on healing by others who have won, and listened to tapes constantly. Our minds were so renewed by the knowledge of the healing goodness of God that we knew we had it. We were going to a Bible Convention that had a session on healing, and I remember a relative said to me, "I hope you get something for Anna there." I couldn't help myself...I yelled out, "We already have it! She is healed! She is whole! She is well in every way! We're just going to hear the Word and to be encouraged, but we already have it!" I shocked myself. Whatever you put in your heart *in abundance* will come out of your mouth. Now, I did not say that to everyone, but it was in my heart in abundance.

Sometimes people tell me they are discouraged because the full manifestation hasn't come. I understand that. We wanted it **now** also, but when you get the healing covenant of God deep within your heart and your mind, you become settled to <u>stand</u> <u>forever</u> and know <u>it will</u> come to pass.

If you are feeling down and discouraged, keep putting the Word in - get that fighting spirit strong! God's promise for healing has already been spoken. He paid for it 2000 years ago. We receive the benefit of that when we hear the Word and believe it. He doesn't have to do or say anything new. It is when we receive what He has already done, by faith, that we receive healing.

Check your conversation. Do you speak in the future? *I believe that someday I'll get my miracle*...That is hope! Faith will always talk the end results, instead of the circumstances at hand or what may exist in the future.

Let's look at Mark 11:24 again: "Therefore I say to you, whatever things you ask when you pray, believe that you receive them, and you will have them." (NKJV) If we believe we receive them, shouldn't that change the way we talk or even pray? Yes! If you believe you have received, you will thank the Lord for the answer; you will talk like you have it.

Confess out loud: *Lord, I thank You for my healing. I thank You for my back being strong again. I can move all around with ease. Lord, I thank You for it.*

The Bible instructs *us* to talk faith. Even *God* talks faith. He always declares something as done, before it is manifested. Romans 4:17 says that **"...even God, who quickens the dead...called those things which be not as though they were."** Paul is referring to Genesis 17 where God said, "I have made you the father of many nations." Notice that God didn't say that He was going to do it. He declared it as done even though Abraham had no children yet. Romans 4:18 says, **"Who against all hope, [Abraham] in hope, believed."** Sometimes we need such a major miracle that it is against all hope to believe for it. In Romans 4:20, we find that Abraham, **"staggered not at the promise of God through unbelief; but was strong in faith, giving glory to God."**

Look at the way God created the earth by speaking it first:

Genesis 1:3 "And God said..."
Genesis 1:6 "And God said..."
Genesis 1:9 "And God said..."
Genesis 1:11 "And God said..."
Genesis 1:14 "And God said..."
Genesis 1:20 "And God said..."
Genesis 1:24 "And God said..."
Genesis 1:29 "And God said..."
Genesis 1:30 "And God **saw** everything that He had made."

Joshua 1:8 says, **"This book of the law shall not depart out of your mouth; but you shall meditate therein day and night, that you may observe to do all that is written therein: for then you shall make your way**

prosperous and then you shall have good success." Here is a formula for success. Success is defined as "obtaining what you set out to do." Success is obtaining the healing you desire. Here, God is telling us to put His Word in our mouths. Think about it day and night. Obey it, and then you will succeed. If you are busy thinking about the Word, like "By His stripes I am healed," and "Don't forget His benefits of healing," then you don't let symptoms overwhelm you.

Proverbs 4:20-23 says, **"My son, attend to my words; consent and submit to my sayings. Let them not depart from your sight; keep them in the center of your heart; for they are life to those who find them; healing and health to all their flesh."** Here again the scripture is telling us to listen to His Word, put it before our eyes, and put it in our hearts (it gets in our hearts by speaking it). Then healing comes. If you have a terminal illness, get the Word of God and good healing tapes to listen to. Write scriptures down to read out loud. Psalm 91:16 says, **"With long life I will satisfy him and show him my salvation."** There is healing in the Word of God.

We are to meditate on the Word and speak it out of our mouths. Then we will have success—the victory we need. Faith is built as we speak God's Word. II Corinthians 4:13 says, **"We having the same spirit of faith according as it is written, 'I believed and therefore <u>have I spoken</u>;' we also believed, and therefore <u>speak</u>...."** *If we believe it, we will speak it.*

Verse 14 says, "While we look not at the things which are seen, but at the things which are not seen; for the things which are seen are subject to change (temporal); but the things which are not seen are eternal." Don't look at the things seen. Don't look at the symptoms, because they are subject to change by the Word of God. Look to the Word. Look to healing in the Spirit and call for it. Eventually, the thing not seen will replace the sickness that is seen.

Job 22:28 says, **"You shall also decree a thing, and it shall be established unto you: and the light shall shine upon your path."** *As we speak God's Word, it is being established in the Spirit. And it will be manifested if we faint not!*

The Bible says that Abraham was **"fully persuaded that what He (God) had promised, He was able to perform"** (Romans 4:21). Just like Abraham, you can be fully persuaded. How did Abraham get fully persuaded? He certainly didn't get that way by saying what the devil said, or what the world said, or what circumstances seemed to be.

Hope says, "I hope for finances to meet my needs."

Faith says, "My God will supply all my needs in Christ Jesus."

Hope says, "I hope I will someday be totally healed."

Faith says, "By His stripes I <u>was</u> healed. I declare today that I <u>am</u> healed, based on the Word of God. Sickness and pain, you leave now!"

Hope says, "I need peace in my life and mind."

Faith says, "If I keep my eyes on You, You keep me in perfect peace. God, You are my peace. My mind and body are at peace in Jesus' name."

The secret to becoming fully persuaded regarding what God has said seems to be in keeping God's Word in our mouths. It is what God told Joshua to do in Joshua 1:8, and in Deuteronomy 28:15 we find a classic example of God teaching Israel how to enter into His promises. **"And it shall come to pass, if you shall <u>hearken diligently</u> unto the voice of the Lord your God, to observe and to do all his commandments which I command you this day, then the Lord your God will set you on high above all nations of the earth: And all these blessings shall come on you and overtake you if you hearken unto the voice of the Lord your God."** "Hearken" in Hebrew means "to hear intelligently, to be obedient, to declare, or to proclaim" (Strong's Concordance). "Diligently" means "wholly, exceedingly, far, fast, and louder and louder" (Strong's).

I like the way one Bible teacher paraphrases this verse: "It shall come to pass, if you shall hear intelligently, be obedient to, declare wholly, completely, far, fast, louder and louder what God has said, observe and to do all His commandments, then all these blessings will come upon you and overtake you."

We may learn to speak words of faith, but miss it on doing God's commandments and abiding in Him. To be honest, I hear people at times say the right words without any power behind them because their personal lives are a mess; there is no real sense of them abiding in Jesus. Their words are a mental assent to the fact that confessing God's Word or calling forth things works, yet they lack God's presence. The Bible says, "Out of the abundance of the heart the mouth speaks" and "If you abide in Me, I'll give you what you ask for." Abiding is more than being disciplined in principles. These principles are scriptural and powerful, but cultivate your prayer relationship with Jesus above all, and then the real power will be released.

CHAPTER 8

Perseverance

"And let us not grow weary in well doing; for in due season <u>we will reap, if we faint not</u>" (Galatians 6:9).

We will reap if we faint not! When you are in a real battle, keep telling yourself, "I will not faint! I will inherit the promises of God!"

Hebrews 6:12 says, "Who through faith and patience inherit the promises." Much of the time, we are going to have to have faith *and* patience working with us. When faith starts to waver because the manifestation is taking a while, patience pushes in and keeps you going until the answer comes.

Patience means, "to be constant or the same way at all times; consistent." That can be very difficult to do if you do not keep your eyes on the Word of God. If with every bad doctor's report, you get all upset and doubt the Word, you will be up and down in your faith. But, if you saturate your mind and heart in the Word of God, you will stay fixed and constant in faith no matter what comes.

When I took Anna Joy to her many doctor's appointments, the ladies at the desk would announce our arrival and whisk us to an isolated room because the virus could infect pregnant women. When a room was not available they would put us in someone's office, and one time they put us in a storage room. It was very painful for us to be treated this way even though we understood their reasons. I would be okay at the appointment, but at times I would get in the car and cry. Fear would try to grip me. The devil would be yelling in my ear, "She is blind, deaf, retarded, and she will never change! God is not answering; your faith isn't working!" My emotions were pressed to the maximum.

But despite the tears and despite the pressure, I would say, "I believe Anna Joy is healed. I refuse to faint. I will inherit the promises of healing." Eventually, as I got stronger in faith, the appointments didn't bother me and neither did the negative reports.

I remember another time in my living room when no one was home except Anna Joy and me. I was studying, listening, and working at building my inner man. All of a sudden tremendous pressure was on me. The neonatologist's voice was racing through my mind: "Send her to the blind center. Get her therapy. Do the drugs..." I knew I had a choice that very day to either give in to the pressure, go the natural way, and never get a miracle, or push through and not give up. The fight of faith seemed too hard. The natural way seemed easier. I did follow much of the doctors' advice, but they didn't have hope or a cure. I needed a miracle. I had to make the choice again to fight the fight of faith.

It can be a real fight; 1 Timothy 6:12 tells us that. There may be times when the pressure is very heavy or the pain is very intense. In these times, I like to visualize a vise grip on the *devil's* head. The more I speak the Word, the tighter it gets, until finally he runs away with all his symptoms. A scripture that helps me in this is Philippians 1:28 (AMP).

You may go out on your back porch and scream or cry, but *don't stay there*. Pull yourself together by the Spirit of the living God and trust Him to see you through to victory!

Remember that "the just shall live by faith!" (Romans 1:17) That means you, the born again believer (the just) lives (speaks, acts, talks, goes about your day) believing God and believing His Word! Live by faith. Be consistent for a long time. Make it your way of life.

Don't just try faith to see if it works. Believe God's Word and live believing Him. Your healing will come.

Faith is believing that you receive whatever you ask, before it can be seen with your senses.

I cannot emphasize enough how important it is to say with your mouth the Word of God OUT LOUD; not in front of a bunch of people because you'll just stir up a bunch of unbelief and confusion, and they will think you are loony. I am talking about in your prayer time, driving in your car, speaking it over your kids as they go to sleep; it's between you and God. Nobody else.

Hebrews 3:1 says, **"Consider the Apostle and High Priest of our profession, Christ Jesus."** The Greek word "profession" is the same as "confession." It means "saying the same thing." Therefore, it means saying what God says about it.

I asked the Lord why we got such a quick breakthrough with Anna Joy. We were prepared to stand a lot longer—years if we had to. We were convinced of God's healing power. God spoke to me and said, "It's because of your mouth." Jeremiah 1:12 says, **"I will hasten My Word to perform it."** When we speak God's Word out loud, I see His angels shooting off to make it come to pass! *Oh, there is power in His Word!*

On the following pages are some healing scriptures. Read these scriptures out loud daily. Meditate on them and let them renew your mind. Let them build faith in you as you speak them out loud. I know the Word of God will be medicine to you as well. As you read them, don't be methodical and religious; make sure your faith is being released in them. The life of God is in them because God's Word is powerful. If it gets old after a while, you might focus on one or two scriptures for a time. Allow the Holy Spirit to lead you.

When I first began to speak out loud over our daughter Anna Joy in my prayer time, I would say, "God, I thank You that Anna is fearfully and wonderfully made. Every organ and cell functions perfectly. You have removed all sickness from her, so CMV has left her body in the Name of Jesus. All its effects have been dissolved by the wonderful power of Jesus. I don't forget the benefits of Jesus being crucified. He forgives my sin and heals all diseases so that Anna's eyes see 20/20 and her ears hear perfectly. Thank You for perfect muscle tone, etc."

I would feel so good after I read the Word and prayed. But then my mind would say, "You are lying." I would have to go back to the Bible and study again. Did Jesus provide healing? Yes, He did. So I would resist that thought and call to mind Romans 4:17, which says, "Even God, Who quickens the dead, called those things which <u>are not</u> as though <u>they were</u>." I knew that I was only calling for what the Bible promised. It is not lying to say what God is saying. He sees things as finished. He sees the end from the beginning. That is His way, so I have to see things that way, too.

Now, if unbelieving people came around, I wouldn't say, "No, nothing is wrong with her," when obviously something was wrong; that would be lying. I would try not to get into a discussion with them, or I would compliment Anna by saying, "Isn't she pretty?" and get away from them if possible. Some would be so rude as to ask, "What's wrong with her?" If I was in a situation where I had to respond, I would state, "She has been diagnosed with CMV, but she is doing wonderfully; she is so sweet," and then go on about how God is strengthening her daily.

What you are constantly saying between yourself and God is more important than a negative conversation with an acquaintance. My sister-in-law Suzanne called while I was learning about "confession" or "calling things that are not as though they were." I was very upset because I seemed to be around a lot of people that were speaking negatively over Anna Joy. I felt like my positive words were competing with the negative words from others. Suzanne pointed out that I was not speaking the Word over Anna for other peoples' benefit, but I was calling for Anna's healing not yet manifest. I was the one with her everyday. My words were the Word and will of God, and they were powerful! Anna Joy's healing may not have been visible in her life yet, but it was true in the Word of God and I was calling for it. It would come!

We were careful not to surround ourselves with people that would get their negative thinking into our heart. My sister Debby and others encouraged us to stay focused and even helped intervene with negative people. I remember one time vividly in the hospital when the neonatologist had just said again the very negative prognosis over Anna Joy. After he left the room, I was crying and my sister Debby said, "I declare those words powerless against her. Our God is a supernatural, healing God." This was especially helpful in the beginning because we were so emotional, and my sister and others who prayed with us did not carry the same pressure we did daily. Ask God to provide faith people to walk with you during your battle. It helps to have others praying and believing with you. We were abrupt at times and probably rude if someone really pushed in to try and be negative. My daughter's life was more important than that person's feelings at the moment. But the people who were negative and thought we were in "denial" cannot argue with a totally healed little girl.

It is so important that we not be religious, but simply believers believing God. Commit to being a learner and a <u>doer</u>. Let go of anything that would keep you from walking with God in all that He has. It's worth it. He's worth it!

God is not a respecter of persons. What God has done for us, He will do for you. He loves you and wants you well. God loves to perform miracles. Even if you are in the middle of waiting for your breakthrough, help others. Pray for hurting people and watch God move through you. You are a miracle. Walk in it!

HEALING SCRIPTURES

Introduction

God is a supernatural God and does move in spectacular ways including healings and miracles. Sometimes we can make the mistake of waiting for Him to do something spectacular and neglect putting His Word in us to do something supernatural.

Proverbs 4:20-22 says, "My son, pay attention to what I say; listen closely to my words. Do not let them out of your sight, keep them within your heart; for they are life to those who find them and health (medicine) to a man's whole body."

God's Word is His Medicine

There are several parallels between God's medicine and natural medicine.

1) God's Word is a healing agent just as natural medicine is a healing agent or catalyst for healing. In other words, the medicine itself contains power to produce healing. Psalm 107:20 says, "He sent His Word, and healed them..." Isaiah 55:10 says that the Word of God will accomplish what it was sent out to do.
2) We might say that medicine is no respecter of persons. It will work for anyone who takes it. Don't get stuck and question whether God wills to heal us. Instead, be at peace and just take the medicine.
3) Medicine must be taken according to directions to be effective. Taking it once in a while when the directions say three times every day will

mean limited results, if any. No matter how good the medicine is, it must be taken according to directions or it will not work. So it is with God's medicine.

The directions for taking God's medicine are found in Proverbs 4:20-21: "My son, give attention to my words; incline your ear to my sayings. Do not let them depart from your sight; keep them in the midst of your heart." We might say that *attending* to them, *inclining* your ear to them, and *keeping* them before your eyes causes them to get into the midst of your heart where they can work healing. Once God's words do penetrate, they will surely bring health to all your flesh.

Here is a list of Scriptures. Feast on them, read them, think about them, talk about them with your friends, pray them as the Spirit leads. This is not meant as a religious habit or ritual but meditating, pondering, getting it inside us where faith rises up in our heart and says "That is my God, He does heal, He is listening, He does move on my behalf". You might find one or two scriptures that really minister to your situation. Memorize that one, or write it on a card to have with you when you get discouraged.

Remember that it takes time for medicine to work. Keep taking God's medicine. Give it time to work. His Word is medicine to all your flesh.

Theme: God will answer when we cry out to Him

Mark 11:24 "Therefore I say unto you, what things you desire, when you pray, believe that you receive them and you shall have them."

John 15:7 "If you abide in Me, and My Words abide in you, ask whatever you will and it shall be done for you."

Matthew 18:19 "Again, I say to you that if any two of you shall agree on earth as touching anything that they shall ask for, it shall be done for them."

Psalm 50:15 "Call on Me in the day of trouble; I will deliver you and you shall honor and glorify Me."

Pray: Lord, I believe Your Word. I am praying today for my total restoration and healing. I believe You hear me and I have my prayer request according to Your Word. *I don't deserve it, but I thank You that it is not based on me deserving it, but based on the payment Jesus made on my behalf. He paid an expensive price for my salvation, healing and deliverance. It is amazing Lord. I receive it by faith and give You all the glory.*

Theme: God helps the attitude of our heart and our countenance

Proverbs 17:22 "A joyful heart is good medicine, but a broken spirit dries up the bones."

Psalm 42:11 "Why are you in despair, O my soul? And why have you become disturbed within me? Hope in God, for I shall yet praise Him, the help of my countenance and my God."

Psalm 91:16 "With long life will I satisfy him, and show him My salvation."

Proverbs 3:1-2 "My son, forget not My law; but let your heart keep My commandments: for length of days, and long life, and peace, they will add to you."

Proverbs 9:11 "For by Me your days shall be multiplied, and your years shall be increased."

Hosea 13:14 "I will ransom them from the power of the grave; I will redeem them from death…"

Pray: *Father, You are good and Your mercies are new every morning. You alone are the giver of life. I believe it is Your will that I live long on the earth and give You glory, to fulfill the number of my days. I command early death to loosen its hold on me and declare that I will live and not die. That the life of God flows through me and all sickness and disease leaves me. Give me Your countenance and the joy of my salvation and deliverance.*

Theme: God removes sickness from us

Exodus 15:26 "And He said, "If you will give earnest heed to the voice of the LORD your God, and do what is right in His sight, and give ear to His commandments, and keep all His statutes, I will put none of the diseases on you which I have put on the Egyptians; for I, the LORD, am your healer."

Deuteronomy 7:15 "The LORD will remove from you all sickness; and He will not put on you any of the harmful diseases of Egypt …"

Exodus 23:25 "But you shall serve the LORD your God, and He will bless your bread and your water; and I will remove sickness from your midst."

Psalm 91:1-6, 10
He who dwells in the shelter of the Most High
Will abide in the shadow of the Almighty.

I will say to the LORD, "My refuge and my fortress,
My God, in whom I trust!"
For it is He who delivers you from the snare of the
    trapper
And from the deadly pestilence.
He will cover you with His pinions,
And under His wings you may seek refuge;
His faithfulness is a shield and bulwark.

You will not be afraid of the terror by night,
Or of the arrow that flies by day;
Of the pestilence that stalks in darkness,
Or of the destruction that lays waste at noon. ...
No evil will befall you,
Nor will any plague come near your tent.

Pray: *Lord Jesus, I want to abide under the shadow of the Almighty. Thank you for forgiving me of all my sins and accepting me completely because of Jesus payment on the cross. You are the one who removes all sickness. You are the one who blesses me. Thank you for removing all sickness from my body. Because of Jesus taking the stripes on His back, I am healed and made whole. Thank you Jesus. I receive my healing today. No evil will befall me, goodness and mercy and long life is my inheritance.*

Theme: God is a healing God

Psalm 30:2 "O LORD my God, I cried to You for help, and You healed me."

Psalm 103:2-3 "Bless the LORD, O my soul, and forget none of His benefits; Who pardons all your iniquities, Who heals all your diseases."

Psalm 107:20 "He sent His word and healed them, and delivered them from their destructions."

Malachi 3:6 "For I am the Lord, I change not..."

Jeremiah 33:17 "For I will restore health to you, and I will heal you of your wounds says the Lord."

Pray: *Lord, I thank You that I can cry out to You when I am in trouble. You not only hear me but You answer. Thank you God that You are a God that does not change. You are just as powerful as You have always been, just as compassionate, loving, and forgiving. I receive Your forgiveness. I receive Your healing and Your deliverance today. Thank you for Your power working on my behalf. I love you Jesus!*

Theme: God heals us in Jesus

Isaiah 53:4-5
"Surely our griefs He Himself bore,
And our sorrows He carried; ...
But He was pierced through for our transgressions,
He was crushed for our iniquities;
The chastening for our well-being fell upon Him,
And by His scourging we are healed.

Isaiah 53:4,5 AMP
Surely He has borne our griefs (sicknesses and diseases), and carried our sorrows (pain): yet we did esteem Him stricken, smitten of God, and afflicted. But He was wounded for our transgressions, He was bruised for our iniquities: the chastisement of our peace was upon Him; and with His stripes we are healed."

1 Peter 2:24 "And He Himself bore our sins in His body on the cross, so that we might die to sin and live to righteousness; for by His wounds you were healed."

Matthew 8:17 "That it might be fulfilled which was spoken by Isaiah the prophet, saying, Himself took our infirmities, and bare our sicknesses."

Psalm 103:2-3 "Bless the Lord, O my soul, and forget not all His benefits; who forgives all our iniquities; who heals all our diseases…"

Pray: *Father I believe Jesus died for my sins and sicknesses according to Your word. Thank you for your great love for me. I believe in my heart and confess with my mouth that you alone are Lord, Savior and Deliverer. Because of Jesus payment on the cross, a very expensive price, I am forgiven, I am healed and I am delivered. I will not forget my benefits not let the enemy steal it from me. I believe and I receive. I am whole, well, and victorious because of Jesus.*

Theme: Healing was a central part of Jesus' mission on earth

Matthew 8:2-3 "And a leper came to Him and bowed down before Him, and said, 'Lord, if You are willing, You can make me clean.' Jesus stretched out His hand and touched him, saying, 'I am willing; be cleansed.' And immediately his leprosy was cleansed."

Mark 5:25-34 "A woman who had had a hemorrhage for twelve years, 26 and had endured much at the hands of many physicians, and had spent all that she had and was not helped at all, but rather had grown worse—after hearing about Jesus, she came up in the crowd behind Him and touched His cloak. For she thought, 'If I just touch His garments, I will get well.' Immediately the flow of her blood was dried up; and she felt in her body that she was healed of her affliction. Immediately Jesus, perceiving in Himself that the power proceeding from Him had gone forth, turned around in the crowd and said, 'Who touched My garments?' And His disciples said to Him, 'You see the crowd pressing in on You, and You say, 'Who touched Me?' And He looked around to see the woman who had done this. But the woman fearing and trembling, aware of what had happened to her, came and fell down before Him and told Him the whole truth. And He said to her, 'Daughter, your faith has made you well; go in peace and be healed of your affliction.'"

Pray: *Jesus, You are the same yesterday, today and forever. The sweet, loving, healing God You were in the Bible You are for me. You have not changed. Thank you for being so moved with compassion on all those people in the Bible. Thank you that Your love, concern and compassion has not diminished. I receive Your love, Your touch today. I move toward You like the woman with the issue of blood. I move toward You like blind Bartemeus. You are healing me, touching me. I receive the healing flow from You into my body now. Thank you Lord for Your healing in my body.*

Theme: Jesus came to destroy the works of the devil

Matthew 8:16-17 "When evening came, they brought to Him many who were demon-possessed;

and He cast out the spirits with a Word, and healed all who were ill. This was to fulfill what was spoken through Isaiah the prophet: 'HE HIMSELF TOOK OUR INFIRMITIES AND CARRIED AWAY OUR DISEASES.'"

Acts 10:38 "You know of Jesus of Nazareth, how God anointed Him with the Holy Spirit and with power, and how He went about doing good and healing all who were oppressed by the devil, for God was with Him."

Romans 8:11 "But if the Spirit of Him who raised Jesus from the dead dwells in you, He who raised Christ Jesus from the dead will also give life to your mortal bodies through His Spirit who dwells in you."

Luke 13:11-13 "And there was a woman who for eighteen years had had a sickness caused by a spirit; and she was bent double, and could not straighten up at all. When Jesus saw her, He called her over and said to her, 'Woman, you are freed from your sickness.' And He laid His hands on her; and immediately she was made erect again and began glorifying God."

1 John 3:8 "... the Son of God appeared for this purpose, to destroy the works of the devil."

1 John 3:8 AMP "… the reason the Son of God was made manifest (visible) was to undo (destroy, loosen, and dissolve) the works the devil (has done)."

Pray: *God, You are a powerful God. No warfare formed against me can prosper! The blood of Jesus covers me and my life, my health, my future. No sickness will stay on my body in Jesus name. Lord, I believe Your*

Word that greater is He that is in me than he that is in the world. Satan cannot defeat me because You are in me. You quicken my body, Your life flows through me. I receive Your victory into my life. Shine through me Jesus. Live through me and grant me a long and healthy life full of honoring You.

Theme: In Christ, we have been given authority over the devil

Luke 10:19 "Behold, I have given you authority to tread on serpents and scorpions, and over all the power of the enemy, and nothing will injure you."

Ephesians 4:27 "… do not give the devil an opportunity."

1 Peter 5:8-9 "Be of sober spirit, be on the alert. Your adversary, the devil, prowls around like a roaring lion, seeking someone to devour. But resist him, firm in your faith …"

James 4:7 "Submit therefore to God. Resist the devil and he will flee from you."

Romans 8:2 "For the law of the Spirit of life in Christ Jesus has set you free from the law of sin and of death."

Galatians 3:13 "Christ redeemed us from the curse of the Law, having become a curse for us — for it is written, 'CURSED IS EVERYONE WHO HANGS ON A TREE…'"

Pray: *Father God, thank You for forgiving me of all my sins. I ask You to forgive me of known and unknown sins in my life. Every way I have sinned against You, I ask for Your forgiveness. Any witchcraft, drug or alcohol* abuse, sexual sins in thought or deeds, any avenue the enemy could enter my life because of my sin, God I ask for Your forgiveness. I ask for forgiveness for the sins of my ancestors, for any way Your name and ways were dishonored. I cut off any generational curses that could pass down to me or my family by faith in the powerful blood of Jesus. By faith I declare that I am free from any attack of the enemy over my body. Any evil spirit attacking me I command you in the name of Jesus to leave my body, leave my mind. Go now in Jesus name, you cannot come against me because I am a child of the King, purchased by Jesus' blood.

Theme: God's Word encourages us to pray for the sick

Mark 16:17-18 "And these signs will follow those who believe: In My name they will cast out demons; they will speak with new tongues; they will take up serpents; and if they drink anything deadly, it will by no means hurt them; they will lay hands on the sick, and they will recover."

Matthew 10:1, 7-8 "And when He had called his twelve disciples to Him, He gave them power over unclean spirits, to cast them out, and to heal all kinds of sickness and all kinds of disease." . . . "And as you go, preach, saying, 'The kingdom of heaven is at hand.' Heal the sick, cleanse the lepers, raise the dead, cast out demons. Freely you have received, freely give."

James 5:14-15 "Is anyone among you sick? Then he must call for the elders of the church and they are to pray over him, anointing him with oil in the name of the Lord; and the prayer offered in faith will restore the one who is sick, and the Lord will raise him up . . . "

Pray: *Lord, I want to obey Your Word, therefore I will go lovingly and compassionately in Your name praying for the sick and proclaiming Your salvation. I trust You to confirm Your Word with signs following that the sick will be healed, the lame will walk, the deaf will hear and we will all give You all the glory. Thank You for moving on behalf of hurting people. You are a good and mighty God.*

2228823

Made in the USA